CHRISTIAN BELIEVING

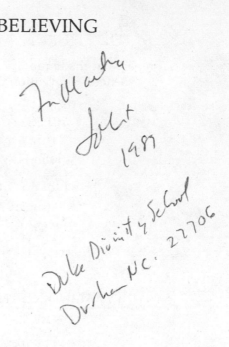

THE CHURCH'S TEACHING SERIES

Prepared at the request of the Executive Council of the
General Convention of the Episcopal Church

CHRISTIAN BELIEVING

Written by
Urban T. Holmes III and John H. Westerhoff III
with the assistance of a group of
editorial advisors under the direction of the
Church's Teaching Series Committee

THE SEABURY PRESS / NEW YORK

1979
The Seabury Press
815 Second Avenue
New York, N. Y. 10017

Printed in the United States of America

Library of Congress Cataloging in Publication Data

Holmes, Urban Tigner, 1930–   Christian believing.

(The Church's teaching series ; v. 1)
Bibliography: p.
Includes index.
1. Apologetics—20th century. 2. Faith.
I. Westerhoff, John H., joint author. II. Title.
III. Series: Church's teaching series ; v. 1.
BT1102.H645   230   79-19607
ISBN 0-8164-0418-6   ISBN 0-8164-2214-1 pbk.

Foreword

The series of books published for the most part in the 1950s and known as the Church's Teaching Series has had a profound effect on the life and work of the Episcopal Church during the past twenty years. It is a monumental credit to that original series and to the authors and editors of those volumes that the Church has seen fit to produce a new set of books to be known by the same name. Though the volumes will be different in style and content, the concern for quality education that prompts the issuing of the new series is the same, for the need of Church members for knowledge in areas of scripture, theology, liturgy, history, and ethics is a need that continues from age to age.

I commend this new Church's Teaching Series to all who seek to know the Lord Jesus and to know the great tradition that he has commended to us.

John M. Allin
PRESIDING BISHOP

THE CHURCH'S TEACHING SERIES

Introduction

This is one of a series of volumes in the new Church's Teaching Series. The project has been both challenging and exciting. Not only is there a wide variety of opinions regarding the substance of the teaching of the Church, there are also varying and conflicting views with regard to the methods of communicating this teaching to others. That is why we have tried to pay close attention to the various movements within the Church, and to address them. The development of this new series, therefore, has involved hundreds of men and women throughout the Episcopal Church and is offered as one resource among many for the purposes of Christian education.

While it is neither possible nor perhaps even desirable today to produce a definitive series of books setting forth the specific teachings of a particular denomination, we have tried to emphasize the element of continuity between this new series and the old. Continuity, however, implies movement, and we believe that the new series breaks fresh ground in a creative and positive way.

The new series makes modest claims. It speaks not so much *for* the Episcopal Church as *to* it, and not to this Church only but to Christians of other traditions, and to those who wait expectantly at the edge of the Church.

Two words have been in constant use to describe this project from its inception: affirmation and exploration. The writers have affirmed the great insights of the Christian tradition and have also explored new possibilities for the future in the confidence that the future is God's.

Alan Jones
CHAIRMAN OF THE
CHURCH'S TEACHING SERIES
COMMITTEE

CHRISTIAN BELIEVING

Contents

· 1 ·

Not by Bread Alone

We live in a society which makes every possible effort to assure us that religion is unnecessary. Perhaps this explains why for more than a century social scientists have predicted the end of religion. Still, no empirical evidence for the decline of religion exists; particular religious communities may come and go but the alleged demise of religion is simply unfounded. Indeed, we appear to be on the brink of a religious revival. Religion in one form or another is an abiding human phenomenon. There appear to be basic longings of the human spirit which nothing else can satisfy and which no human effort can finally suppress: humans cannot live by bread alone. Human life requires some sort of religion for survival.

When we use the word religion we are not talking about what *you* believe as compared to what *we* believe: Protestantism vs. Catholicism, Christianity vs. Hinduism. We are speaking of a motivating force similar to hunger. Humans, it appears, are by nature religious beings; they have an innate longing for cosmos, or order, in life's chaos.

Americans live in the presence of a great historic irony. Never have a people known a greater degree of economic security, social mobility, and educational opportunity; never have they had as great a potential for living long, healthy lives. At the same time, never a day passes that we are not in some way confronted by a gloomy depiction of the human condition. Few thinking people would be particularly surprised to learn that recently a group of high school students,

1

when asked to write their first English papers, chose to write on the theme of their individual discovery of the precariousness of existence, their awareness that life can be cut off at any moment without warning, and their simultaneous discovery that the grown-up world (father and mother) cannot make everything all right.

Chaos appears to be an ever present human experience—but an experience most humans cannot bear. Humans innately respond to the threat of chaos by a thrust toward cosmos—that ideal of order where everything is arranged in proper relationship to everything else and the whole appears to be good, beautiful, and true. Humans are essentially religious because they possess a need for order, a need to make sense out of their lived experience, and a need to find answers to those questions most people eventually ask: Is there meaning to life in general and to my life in particular? What is my purpose? Does anybody care what happens to me?

The desire to moor our lives to some sort of ultimate meaning is as natural as eating. Ingmar Bergman, the Swedish film-maker, was quoted as saying, in effect, that "life without God is unbearable." Bergman, in this case, was neither affirming nor promoting a belief in the existence of God; he was suggesting that humans cannot live productively without some sense of an overarching meaning for life.

As the French philosopher Maurice Merleau-Ponty wrote, "Because we are present to the world, we are condemned to meaning." No matter how meaningless life may seem to be, as long as we live our humanity tells us that life must have meaning. That is why we are haunted and driven until we can discover this meaning and live accordingly.

The secret of the human life is not so much to live, as to live for something. Albert Camus, the French playwright and novelist, has suggested that it does not, after all, matter very much whether the earth goes round the sun or the sun goes round the earth—the only really serious question is whether, either way, our life is or is not worth living. In Paris in 1968, a time of student unrest, these words were painted on the walls of the University of Paris, *"survivre n'est pas vivre"* (survival isn't living). There simply has to be more to life than the vicissitudes of daily existence. To live is to search for ultimate meaning.

Religion, then, is best understood as both the quest for, and the response to that which is truly ultimate. By ultimate we mean that which is fundamental to life, that which transcends the superficial world of provable fact, that which leads to some sense of a total experience in which we find a resolution for our lives, a sense of order, a mooring, and a meaning. As such, religion is more than a concern for the immediate; it seeks to find or to discover an authentication for all experience: past, present, and future.

Religious Experience

There are, of course, people who would deny that they have a need for religion. Often these are people who live for the moment, making the issues of meaning or purpose senseless. And there are those who deny that they have any natural drive toward the religious. These people are so absorbed in the successful business of everyday life that they have no time for ultimate questions. But the experience of the human race across time and culture, as well as the contemporary experience of many people, reveals a very different understanding. We humans, whether we want to admit it or not, are, in the final analysis, religious.

In the summer of 1978 a television documentary reported on a sampling of life as lived by some people in Marin County, California—a prosperous suburban community just across the Golden Gate Bridge from San Francisco. The report was principally an analysis of an unfeeling, self-centered group who pursued their own immediate pleasures with little concern for the future or for anyone else. It would not have been newsworthy if it has not been offensive to what most of us value: living for the future, living for others. Similarly, Colin M. Turnbull's analysis of a dislocated African tribe, the Ik, entitled *The Mountain People* (1972), was, as books on anthropology go, a best-seller. Why? Because Turnbull described the life-style of a people who, like those in the documentary about Marin County, abandoned their children, left the old to die uncomforted, and robbed the weak to satisfy their own momentary pleasure. We read the story of the Ik in fascinated horror, wondering how a people could move so far from those values we believe to be essential to life. Such values are ultimately religious.

Nevertheless, it is difficult to describe religious attitudes. In one sense religiousness is too personal and dynamic to be described analytically. But if we are to share and examine that which is deepest and most profound in our lives, it is essential to try.

One way that people have expressed their religiousness is by describing an experience of what can be best identified as the holy—that profound sense that there is infinitely more to experience than we can explain. The word "holy" points toward that which transcends or eludes comprehension, toward an awareness beyond our ordinary perceiving or conceiving. At best we can describe this awareness as mysterious, recalling that the word "mystery" expresses a sense of ignorance deeper than that which can be dispelled by information. Indeed, its proper referent is *radical* ignorance or that which we not only *do* not know, but *cannot* know through any usual means.

Human awareness of the religious stretches from records in painting and sculpture of the lives of early cave dwellers to the essays of contemporary theoretical scientists. Each describes in unique ways a dimension of life's experience that is best summarized in this way: If we look within ourselves we begin to see that our identity is dependent on something deeper than ourselves; it is like peeling away the layers of an onion—we eventually come to the inside; we find ourselves dependent upon that which is dependent upon nothing else; it is a feeling of absolute dependence in the presence of something which is of infinite worth or value.

It seems that the human mind is disposed not only to rationality, but also to spiritual awareness, an experience of both fascination and terror. When we acknowledge our ultimate finiteness and give over our lives to what is beyond our control, then we experience a sense of the sacred. To be conscious of ourselves as creatures before a creative force or energy is to apprehend the religious dimension of life.

Another way people have described their religiousness is by pointing to the basic assumptions upon which all human life is lived. To be human is to assume that there is order in the universe to be discovered, trusted, and accepted. When the great nineteenth-century astronomer Joseph Leverrier was confronted with what appeared to be meaningless irregularities in the orbit of the planet Uranus, his faith in the basic order of the universe was so great that he asserted that there had to be a reason for the irregularities. And so he went looking for it, and discovered Pluto, a hitherto unknown planet, which was causing the seemingly meaningless irregularities in the orbit of Uranus. The pursuit of life's order is as natural as breathing. And despite life's seeming chaos we discover with a resulting sense of awe and wonder that it has order.

Some people have described their religiousness through a discovery of the limits of language. We know that we are only fully conscious of that which we can represent. Language is necessary to bring to full consciousness what we experience. Yet as we try to express our experience of life's meaning, we are aware that our consciousness points beyond the limits of our language—beyond what we can say or imagine saying.

Over the last two hundred years Western civilization has struggled to comprehend the human phenomenon. Through the rise of the human sciences—psychology, sociology, economics, political science, anthropology—we have attempted to explain what being human is like. Our efforts have expanded our conscious knowledge greatly. But we still have not really plumbed the depths of the unconscious. We do not really understand what we were before we were born, and death remains for humans the final unknown. We are like a spot of brilliant light surrounded by the pitch black of our ignorance. We cannot rest content with the light; we seek to probe into the dark, to express what lies beyond our grasp. The only language available to us is that of symbol or metaphor (a figure of speech in which a word or phrase literally denoting one object or idea is used in place of another to suggest a likeness or analogy between them). To acknowledge the limits of our language makes us aware of our religiousness.

Our religiousness is that which is experienced in the midst of our humanness as the holy, that which is beyond expression except in the language of symbols, that which gives us a sense of order in the apparent chaos of life. Our religion provides us with a spiritual center of security and meaning; it provides roots of stability, coherence, and direction for our lives. Amid all our concerns, those concerns founded in religious faith demand a total surrender and, in return, promise to provide ultimate fulfillment. Destroy this center and most people are overcome by a radical anxiety. When a religious center is present, we possess hope and confidence—even in the most severe assault on life's meaning.

Two Types of Religion

This explanation of religion and the religious may seem somewhat confusing and even irrelevant to the vitality of the personal religious experience many people have and its resultant life-giving power. The purpose, however, in describing the human experience was to indicate the depth and breadth of religiousness as well as the necessity of vital religion in human culture. It is important to understand that living religiously is an attribute of personhood. However, what is perhaps more important is to acknowledge that this human longing for religious meaning can express itself in either negative or positive ways. Religion, while natural and necessary to human life, is not always in every expression to be valued or affirmed.

Religion has sometimes been attacked quite legitimately as supportive of what many people discern as the worst in human nature: intolerance, bigotry, sentimentality, self-righteousness, neurotic fantasy, rigidity, ignorance, and pride. At its worst religion, which should embody "perfect freedom," can become a form of slavery. Sociologists of religion have shown, for example, that unimaginative and restrictive "orthodoxy" (rigid adherence to the classical teachings of historic Christianity) can be linked to racism and a general insensitivity to human suffering. Suppression of the truth in the name of God has been all too common in human history. The question for some contemporary people is whether religion is a symptom of human sickness or necessary to our health.

It is important, therefore, to distinguish between two functional types of religion, one that is inclined to support health and one that is inclined to support sickness. Both make an appeal to ultimate goals. Both are beyond the limits of language and embodied in symbols. And both are perceived as holy. But they diverge quite radically and serve essentially conflicting functions in the lives of people and society. Ironically, both types of religion can be present in a single individual or in a single community. The first type of religion might be called "the religion of involvement" and the second type "the religion of escape."

THE RELIGION OF INVOLVEMENT

Religion can be a healthy response to life. When religion serves our human strengths, it is best understood as engaging us in life's struggles, as being rational, and as being expressive of inner control or self-direction.

A religion of involvement is dedicated to the pursuit of meaning and value in human life. Aware that the world can not meet our deepest needs, religion becomes an instrument for our progressive strivings after a sense of transcendent purpose for life. Just as important, it becomes a catalyst directing our lives toward a vision of a better life. It looks to the future and uses the past as leverage to move toward that future. Tradition is alive and provides a guide toward working with God to make creation anew.

There is no discomfort in the idea that God is a surprise. A religion of escape is easy; its demands are superficial; it gives the believer the illusion of safety. A religion of involvement is difficult and risky; its demands are profound; it points the pilgrim to a dark and dangerous road. It offers not safety but an opportunity to find new and unexpected maturity. Its adherents do not use the church and its liturgy for escape and comfort, but for challenge and empowerment. Their concern is not to judge or convert people who believe differently, but to live faithfully with them. Acknowledging their own acceptance and adequacy, their concerns are the world and the struggle for justice.

This type of religion meets the challenge of the intellect head-on. While it does not assert that one can know God by the power of one's mind, it certainly accepts reason and its cultivation as a gift of God. Beliefs are accepted only after they appear reasonable. These believers do not assume that there is a conclusive proof for the existence of God. Nor do they seek for a rational explanation of their experience which "explains" it all. They are simply aware that the more they push back the horizons of their knowing, the more aware they are of the infinite *more* to be explored.

They, therefore, live with a childlike openness to the *more* that lies beyond our perception and reason. They strive to perceive the subject that lies beyond their experience. For these open-minded people, reason and emotion, intellect and intuition, are all aspects of human life and essential for religious discovery. Still they seek to study seriously religion and the religious. And they subject their religious convictions to a thorough intellectual analysis.

As might be expected, these people are self-directed. While they do not know all the answers and do not have an authoritarian source for their beliefs, attitudes, and actions, they consciously strive to act morally. They have internalized norms for life consistent with their beliefs, and principles to be used as they rationally attempt to mediate between their norms and the moral situations in which they find themselves.

Someone who "has it all together," is one who we would say has a strong ego. Those with a "religion of involvement" have strong egos; they can face challenges, live in ambiguity and with change, and still maintain their equilibrium as they willingly move into the unknown as a necessary condition of growth. This does not mean that they are free from fear, but that they fear the numbing results of enslavement to the status quo more than they fear the change and uncertainty that go with personal and spiritual growth.

Such an understanding of religion is founded upon revelation rather than magic. Revelation is an openness to that which is hidden. It is the apprehension of experience as a whole, the affirmation of a fundamental power in society and nature for good, and the perception that life has an ultimate purpose. Religion as revelation is an invitation into fuller humanity, an attempt to bring human life into harmony with God's will rather than to manipulate the world for one's own benefit. It is the religion of a Dag Hammerskjold, a Martin Luther King, Jr., or a Dorothy Day.

The religion of involvement is an inclusive believing which takes the whole of human experience seriously. It draws and pushes us into the unknown that we may try to become that person who exists, truly, only in the mind of God. It provides the assurance which enables us to become vulnerable and to risk death. It fears no truth and is firmly convinced that truth is to be found in laboratories as well as churches, in the novels of atheists as well as in the lives of the saints. It despises nothing that God created and knows sin, not in terms of arbitrary labels, but in the uncertain light of what destroys our potential humanity. It insists that for religion there is no division of "sheep and goats" in terms of private and public, in-race and out-race, male or female, or rich and poor. It is a religion necessary for human health.

THE RELIGION OF ESCAPE

Some religion can serve human weakness. When it does, it is best understood as an escape from life, as an irrational emotional longing, and as an expression of an unconscious desire for parental authoritarianism.

For some people religion can be a support or protection from those dimensions of their lives in which they feel inadequate. Participation in the liturgy, while therapeutic, can be escapist, that is, it can make it possible to live with an unquestioned individual and social life. Membership in a prominent parish can give a person a sense of status and importance. To be offered multiple responsibilities in the church, regardless of their significance, is to acquire significance for oneself. If we are inclined to think of ourselves as inferior, a strict religious community with clear demands or beliefs that set us apart (no drinking, no dancing, and the like) can assure us that we are better than others if we are able to live up to those beliefs. At least we can be confident of a heavenly reward, which others, who may have "made it" in this life, cannot share.

These same people are typically unwilling to subject their religious convictions to intellectual analysis. Indeed, they often possess a strong anti-intellectual bias. They reject the question of whether or not their religious beliefs are reasonable. For them all that matters is a unique emotional experience. It is common for these people to hold the conviction that if people study religion seriously they will "lose their faith." A learned priest is someone to be avoided, as is serious adult education. These people typically protect themselves and their beliefs from attack and possible dissolution by resisting all logical scrutiny. Literalism, whether biblical, dogmatic, ethical, or liturgical, always seems to prevail among these close-minded adherents of fundamentalistic religion.

Further, those people with a "religion of escape" suffer from an unconscious wish for parental authoritarianism. They *know* the answers or have access to the answers because of an infallible authoritarian source which they project on God, the Bible, or the church. These people have often stopped growing at an emotional level in which they require an authoritarian parent to resolve the terror of life's uncertainty. God becomes a defense against the unknown, the conflicts and ambiguities of life. The very rigidity of such an authority is an assurance that they are safe.

Religion for these people is typically understood as magic or as the means by which they can achieve their desires by praying long and hard enough or by performing some other act of piety. It is a coercive, controlling, and manipulative vision of religion. Through the exercise of religion they seek to control life for their purposes. Through religious practices, they attempt to manipulate and control a parental authority through irrational means so they can cope with and control their essentially escapist world. It is in this sense that religion has sometimes been considered the "opiate of the people."

Clearly a religion of escape is defensive; it aims to protect one from alien forces. It is a safe harbor in a sea of storms. It comforts and provides peace of mind. Such a religion is functionally effective because it gives answers and leaves no questions. This also means that it is intolerant, moralistic, dogmatic, and rigid. Truth is known. One accepts it or rejects it; there is no continuing revelation. It is a religion of exclusion. It must by nature divide people into "we" and "they," at best considering the "they" as unenlightened and in error and at worst shunning and condemning them to hell. It supports bigotry, self-righteousness, repression, and even violence. Such a religion feeds on the need to be better than others and grows rapidly in times of uncertainty and cultural change. A religion of this sort can contribute to human (individual and corporate) sickness.

A Temptation and Challenge

Mature, healthy religion necessarily seeks a positive interaction between personal belief and the public world. It honors the hard work of critical examination, assuming that Christian believing is both plausible and reasonable. It desires to engage in intellectual analysis because it is convinced that this activity is necessary if the church is to be taken seriously and provide an effective moral witness to the world.

If we attempt to avoid the interaction between personal belief and the world, if we avoid engaging in conceptual thought aimed at enlightenment and action, then we are involved in an unjustifiable effort designed to mystify or bewilder. Healthy religion will always support and be expressive of mystery. But healthy religion will avoid that sense of false mystery, which sanctions our escape from the enigmas of life and from moral witness and which sick religion encourages.

Perhaps some illustrations of a false appeal to mystery will help. If we believe that God is all-powerful (can do anything), knows everything (even what will happen in 2000), and is everywhere, what do we make of such a tragic event as this? A couple has a daughter who is about to graduate from college with a 4.0 average. She is beautiful, active in the church, and has the promise of a very good job. A week before commencement she is killed in an automobile accident—hit by a drunk. The couple asks their priest, "How can an all-powerful, all-knowing, all-present God let this happen?" Well aware that to say, "It is God's will," is to make God out to be at best a kind of despot and, at worst, and more likely, a deranged monster, the priest replies, "The ways of God are a mystery." Such an answer refuses to deal with the doctrine of providence in today's world. Instead of examining, in the light of our contemporary understandings of appropriate moral behavior, the notion of free will, that of the girl who was killed, the drunken driver, and even that of the inventor of the internal combustion engine, the priest is *escaping* into a pseudo-mystery and is asking us to do the same.

For another example we can imagine a workshop on "experiental theology." In this workshop the leader, by means of music, meditative techniques, color slides, and body movement seeks to create a setting where we may come to a profound sense of God's presence in our lives. At the end of the exercise he says, "No one should talk to anyone else about what may have happened to him. Let us just 'live' this journey together into the symbolic world. The presence of God is always a mystery; to talk about it destroys the sense of this presence." Does it sound farfetched? Some have said that Christians should only dance their belief and avoid theological reflection. To put religious ideas in the form of theology, some believe, is to make belief meaningless and uninteresting. We would reply that in such a workshop setting a person may only have had, at best, an aesthetic experience. The only way such an experience can be distinguished from religious experience is by critical analysis.

A false appeal to mystery is always a temptation. For example: A priest might explain the heart of his or her parish ministry in this way. "We are an altar-centered parish. We come from all walks of life and every human condition. Every Sunday we gather about the Lord's table and eat the bread and drink the wine of the Lord. We look across at one another, and we find oneness. I do not ask what this means, because that will only divide us into theological camps. I just know that we have experienced the mystery that is God." There is something very appealing about this on one level: but what difference does it make on Monday morning? We need poetry in our religious lives, but we must also have prose. A false sense of mystery, while it may avoid arguments, also prevents us from dealing with the day-to-day implications of our belief.

In the first example, by ordinary standards an event is either purposeful, caused by the direct action of an agent, or else it is mere chance and illustrative of the absurdity of life. It means nothing to say it is a mystery. Theology has to face the darkness of death, not illuminate it artificially with platitudes that lie to our experience.

The leader of the workshop in the second illustration is suggesting that the meaning of religious experience wilts under the light of critical analysis. He, like the priest who wants to say it is just a mystery, believes that theology is alien to religious experience.

In the third illustration, the priest intentionally refuses to allow his ministry to go beyond the symbols and the story. In all of these illustrations, we see the tendency of false mystery to divide reality into the ordinary and the extraordinary, natural and supernatural, profane and sacred. This tendency leads ultimately to the division of private faith and public life. This division is contrary to the church's experience of Jesus.

Mystery is not to be removed from religion, only *false* mystery. Of course, the very nature of theology could be called a reduction into mystery. The believer who is thinking about God and humanity in a disciplined way—a good definition of theology—knows that the truth of anything said about God is conditioned upon our willingness to let that statement extend beyond our comprehension into the silent mystery of God. The silence, however, is not the answer, but the problem. We continue to probe that silence even though we understand that it is not possible for the finite to fully comprehend the infinite. Religion's positive interaction with the public world demands that we engage in a penetrating critical analysis of all our attempts to express in words and ideas our religious experience and faith.

· 2 ·

What Can We Believe?

Faith is our natural human orientation toward life's ultimate meaning and purpose. As such, faith is universal and ever present. But belief is the content of our faith and thereby ever-changing. Faith asks, "Is there a God?"; belief answers, "This is God." Today all persons of religious faith face a similar crisis—the anxiety of being unable to believe in the same way our grandparents or great-grandparents believed.

In the tenth century people understood the world as a reflection of the mind of God. In the sixteenth century the Reformers taught that the Scriptures made God's mind accessible to all faithful readers. The philosophers of the seventeenth and eighteenth centuries explained that the fundamentals of belief were available to all through reasonable inquiry into the data of experience. Today many seem to find themselves in sympathy with the last century's suggestion that belief requires a leap of trust in the face of contrary evidence.

"Keep the faith, baby!" was an admonition of blacks during the racial turmoil of the 1960s. What did it mean? What was the "faith" to which they appealed and called their brothers and sisters to keep? Surely it was not a body of orthodox doctrinal teachings. There were no sacred writings of the black culture which their leaders called upon the community to defend. It was a plea to keep trust in the movement and not to lose sight of an awareness of their present condition nor of the possibility offered by life for an alternative. In all the struggle, the pain, and the uncertainty, the speaker was reciting what amounted to a litany for the keepers of the "faith" to persist.

It is important to distinguish between *faith* and *belief*. Religious faith is an attribute of personhood. As long as we have records of humanity we have records of religious faith. Faith, deeply personal, dynamic, and ultimate, has always been present among all peoples at all times in history.

Faith—the word appears two hundred and thirty-three times in the Authorized Version of the Bible (belief appears only once)—is best understood as fidelity, as trusting obedience. Faith implies a deliberate and positive existential involvement; it precedes belief.

The word for belief in Latin is *opinio*. "To believe" is *opinor, opinari*—that is, to have an opinion or to make an intellectual assertion.

Credo should never have been translated as belief. The only reason it was so translated is that in classical theology, faith and belief were considered synonymous. In any case, *credo* literally means "I set my heart." To have religious faith—*credo*—is to pledge allegiance, to hold dear, to prize, to love intimately, to give our loyalty, to commit our lives.

Faith can be and indeed must be expressed in words and ideas. *Beliefs are intellectual expressions of a people's faith.* But beliefs are *not* faith. Traditionally, theology has said that seekers ask two basic questions: First, "Is there a God?"—a question which demands a simple "yes or no" answer; *faith* is the affirmative response. Second, "What is God?"—a question of *belief* whose answer is complex, diverse, and always inadequate.

Faith is like falling in love. But suppose you are the father of an adolescent daughter, with a typical, built-in suspicion of all her suitors. Your daughter tells you that she is "in love" with a man, but that is not enough. If you are like most fathers, you want more than that. You ask: Tell us what he is like. What you are asking for is a statement of belief.

Your daughter will probably have a very difficult time relating the reality of her love to the request that she describe him *as he has "related" to her* (which is the only way anyone can describe another). In fact, it may be considered a blessing that one person cannot really describe to another what they have experienced to be true about their beloved. If they could, the person listening to their experience might gain the same "faith" in the beloved. This conversion would have a very complicating effect: the person hearing about their friend's beloved would be as deeply in love with the one described as the friend doing the describing! The same is true about God. Relatively few people come to have faith in God solely because they read a book of theology, which is, of course, someone's description of what they personally perceive God to be.

Another way of defining religious belief is to say it is what we _predicate_ of God. If you are over twenty-five (language study has changed), somewhere in your schooling you must have studied "predicate nominatives" and "predicate adjectives." They are nouns and adjectives that follow a verb and are descriptive of the subject. To say "Jesus is the Son of God" is to _predicate_ divinity of Jesus. "Son of God" is a predicate nominative. To say that "God is good" is to _predicate_ goodness of God. "Good" is a predicate adjective. Both of these statements answer the second question—they state _what_ God is. They are belief statements, rather than faith statements. A faith statement would be "God is" (that is, God exists), which has no predication.

We are making the distinction between faith and belief because we want to argue that faith has an _absolute_ and _universal_ quality that belief does not.

By "absolute" it would seem that at a given point in time you either are _in faith_ or you are not. There is a "yes or no" quality to faith. You can no more possess half-faith than you can be half-pregnant. Faith does not permit you to "hedge your bets." You affirm the existence and integrity of God or you do not, even if you do the former as a kind of "wager."

Faith is eternal. Our beliefs are bound to time and place. Our beliefs are relative to our history. Faith is shared by humanity through the ages, but our beliefs are expressed in each age, in pluralistic ways, in the context of the culture in which we live.

Nevertheless, while believing and beliefs may differ from

one century to another, the need to believe remains as crucial as ever. To believe is as essential to humans as are air and water to all living things, and as fundamental as loving. In the 1950s President Eisenhower was ridiculed by some theologians because he said that he thought everyone ought to believe something, but he did not care what they believed. To a point he was right. Humans need to believe so that they may make their faith a conscious and living thing and express for themselves and others their understanding of life's meaning and purpose. But *what* we believe is also very important because it determines how we act. For example, there is no question but that those who murdered six million Jews during World War II were acting in accord with what they believed. It is essential for all persons of faith in every age to reexamine their believing and their beliefs.

It is not easy to interpret an era. As a matter of fact, it is all but impossible to describe the American religious situation today. Still, while tremendous variety abounds, people have a strong drive to express verbally what they believe or to have a spokesperson say it for them. This cry is a haunting and poignant one in a world in which there are almost as many different beliefs as there are people. However, it is important to acknowledge and address those beliefs which challenge Christianity if we are to believe faithfully. We have isolated six types of belief which confront Christianity: pluralism; religious neutrality; technocracy; materialism; pietism; and atheism—intellectual, moral, linguistic, and social.

Pluralism

Pluralism—a social order founded upon the principle of harmonious interaction, for common ends, among various distinct communities—is a central affirmation of our democratic society. By the close of the colonial period our nation was acknowledged to be religiously diverse. When the colonies won their freedom from England, the framers of the Constitution, fired with the ideas of the Enlightenment, were determined to avoid a state religion in any form. This allowed religious diversity to flourish—and to grow—in the

United States. Interaction between and among the various religious traditions has both increased and been encouraged.

Diverse ideologies confront most Americans every day. The melting pot concept of America, although founded on good intentions, has always been a fiction. The best we have achieved is open dialogue between persons representing different cultures. The results have sometimes been traumatic. The smorgasbord of ideologies that confront modern Americans, each seeking an allegiance and loyalty, is disconcerting. To be driven to see that all truth may finally be subjective, at least in the sense that it is shaped by our inevitable cultural biases, is indeed troubling.

Everyone is born into a community and learns that community's beliefs, attitudes, and values. Then at a very early age we are confronted by persons and groups who have been shaped by *their* communities into radically different understandings and ways. To complicate matters, each of these communities claims truth for their particular convictions. Further, they seek overtly to convince us that their beliefs are more true than our own. A crisis in identity ensues. Eventually we may well come to question the credibility of all belief.

Today many people, in order to maintain a necessary set of beliefs by which to live, make all belief subjective and say, in effect, "all that matters is what I believe and do." In this situation, universal principles and norms for conduct are replaced by private, contextual decision-making. Public beliefs, essential for economic, social, and political life, are often framed in terms of a lowest common denominator. All truth becomes relative. Life becomes a "private" matter. The sharp clashing of private belief and the social world diminishes. Religious belief becomes an especially private affair, experienced in a very individual way, and expressed in isolation from the world.

Surely pluralism is valuable, but the complete isolation of individuals in matters of belief and, actually, in every meaningful aspect of their lives, is socially destructive. While it is through the interaction of diverse communities that growth and change are made possible, pluralism makes believing and the need to test personal beliefs against public beliefs trying and difficult. The typical reaction of many people in a pluralistic society is to avoid this interaction and permit belief to recede into a private consciousness. When this occurs a special burden is placed upon believing.

Religious Neutrality

Nonbelief has become the law of the land. The need for national unity has turned the commitment of the nation's founders to freedom *for* religious identity in an open society—the principle expressed in the doctrine of separation of church and state—into freedom *from* religious identity on behalf of civil harmony. The United States Constitution in recent years has been consistently interpreted to mean that the state is in no way to contribute to any particular affirmation of religious belief. As a matter of fact, our society does not even support the contention that a commitment to belief is preferable to disbelief.

Aside from curious anomalies (and they may not last much longer) such as coins which state "In God We Trust" and a pledge of allegiance which affirms " . . . one nation under God. . ." we have, in effect, affirmed a legal nonbelief.

In the early days of our nation church-supported schools, with clear religious identities and orientations, were considered important means of helping people live in a genuinely new world. But soon the public support of church-related schools was denied. A national commitment to the education of the public became identified with public education. The state's right and duty to encourage education had become the right and duty to educate. As soon as that fateful decision was made, the state and its educational institutions moved toward neutrality on all matters of religious significance. The result has been a functional elimination of religion from its original place of central importance in our national life.

Passionate religious believing is simply not supported any longer in our society. There is a striking example of the very different attitude of earlier Americans to be found in a passage from the *Annals of Congress* devoted to the trial of Aaron Burr. On November 23, 1807 Burr was arraigned with this citation: "Aaron Burr . . . not having the fear of God before his eyes . . . but being moved and seduced by the instigation of the devil, wickedly devising and intending the peace and tranquility of the said United States to disturb did . . . ." Here the civil court felt it important to offer a clear theological explanation of Aaron Burr's treason. His sin was a result of his vulnerability to the devil and of the devil's active pursuit of his soul, they said. Some of us may still hold that to be true, but it is very unlikely that such a theological reflection would be tolerated in a public document today. A recent interview of members of Congress revealed that they saw their own decision-making as "political" rather than "moral" or "religious." Life has become less whole.

Moreover, our major informal sources of education—the mass media—present us with cultural heroes who lend little support by their examples to the importance of believing. The television programs with the highest viewer ratings, the movies with largest attendance, and the paperback books sold in largest numbers generally do not offer us examples for living which have a coherent understanding of the meaning and purpose of human life.

In a nation where nonbelief is forcefully encouraged, the difficulty of believing is clear.

Technocracy

Our culture is best understood from a technological perspective. For the first time in human history earth's whole environment has been permeated by, and to a large extent controlled by, mechanical devices. We live in a world of technique, control, and prediction. It is a world of means rather than ends. The ubiquitous computer and the almost equally ubiquitous automobile—a necessity, it would seem, from teenager on—have become dominant symbols of our age. There is also general enthusiasm for anything new and an apparent need to control and predict. Control and predict what? Everything. Is it any wonder that people are inclined increasingly to discredit or forget what is eternal, surprising, and uncontrollable?

In a society with a technocratic consciousness there is little need for religious beliefs. Indeed, the question of what happens to us and to our world ultimately is considered unimportant. Therefore it is not surprising that behaviorism, in one form or another, has become the dominant philosophy of psychologists. Behaviorism asks only why people behave as they do. All social processes, behaviorism asserts, can be reduced to the behavior of individuals deterministically understood. To speculate on consciousness or will as forms of self-knowledge and actualization is considered a waste of time and energy.

Behaviorism may supply a satisfactory world view for a culture dominated by technology, but consider what happens to believing when we perceive that only the observable and measurable are real. Consider further the implications of the conviction that all reality can be divided into discrete, manageable components. Is this not to say that God, if God exists, is unknowable? Does this position not imply that we have to live as if there is no God, whether or not this contention is true? Scientific positivism, which undergirds our technological culture, simply argues that we can claim to know only that which we can verify in a particular manner. At best we can say, "I cannot state that I believe in God but I have found that the only way to avoid despair is to live as if I believed."

While our technocratic society has provided us with numerous beliefs, and both scientific positivism and behaviorism have made possible important insights into natural and human behavior, they also present significant problems for believing and belief.

MATERIALISM

We have been blessed, or some would say cursed, with material abundance. We live in an acquisitive society, a society in which possession of things is dominant. The supreme goal of our culture is to have.

Possession, ownership, property, greed for money and things characterize our lives. Even our language, once dominated by the verb, has witnessed an increased use of the noun—a denotation for a thing. We say we *have* a problem; *have* a job; *have* a degree; *have* friends; and we even *have* a lover. The *it* of having has replaced the *I* of intimacy and experience.

Because our society values acquiring property and making a profit, most of us have come to assume that the "having" mode of existence is a natural, normal, and acceptable way of life. So prevalent is this attitude that for many of us the claim that we "have" or "own" our bodies and can, therefore, seek an abortion without any moral issue being raised is challenged with much less frequency than formerly. Believing in this "having" mode is therefore typically understood as possessing answers formulated by others and accepted on the authority of those in power—the same basis upon which a materialistic culture is inclined to formulate all value. Of course having beliefs given to us by others carries a feeling of certainty, for it relieves us of the hard task of thinking for ourselves and making decisions. We are the happy owners of the right and proper set of beliefs.

However, we cannot *have* God. Nor can we possess ultimate, eternal, unquestionable beliefs. As humans we are always being and becoming, formulating and reformulating our beliefs. *Being* rather than having is basic to our human nature. The difference between having and being is at the heart of the religious life.

The Buddha taught that to arrive at the highest level of human development we must *be* rather than crave possessions. Even Karl Marx taught that the goal of the truly human life is to be much and to become much. And Jesus taught us that those who seek to save (possess) their lives will lose their lives. In this being mode, belief is the rational explanation of an inner attitude or orientation. But it is not easy to believe in this religious sense in a world dominated by materialism and having.

Pietism

Anti-intellectualism has always been present in American culture. While we spend millions of dollars on education, education is typically understood as having value because it is a means to an end, the way we reach another goal—a job, for example. Americans are not inclined to think of education, the gaining of knowledge, as an end in and of itself. The intellectual quest for truth is not seriously valued in our culture. Those who pursue it are considered somewhat strange if not impractical. People who make thinking and thought a priority in their lives are often characterized as "egg heads." Those who can produce practical, usable goods and services are usually paid more than philosopher-theologians. Entertainers, comedians, popular musicians, and athletes are considered of greater value than the people who make up the humanities faculty of a university.

In the world of religion this distrust of reason may often take the form of pietism. Pietism, which is emotional but not intellectual, seems, in many ways, to dominate American culture. Historically, pietism may be seen as a reaction to a sterile theology. It has appeared in this guise in the fifteenth, late seventeenth, and, it seems, in the late twentieth centuries. Fundamentalistic evangelicalism, Pentecostal charismatics, Eastern mystic cults—all, more often than not, place the affections ahead of the intellect. And these religious groups, with their strong emphasis on feelings, on the religion of the heart, are inevitably more popular than those faiths which affirm thought, or the religion of the head. Believing, unless it is understood as the blind emotional acceptance of dogmatic convictions, will always have difficulty in the presence of pietism.

Indeed, among many pietists, to think seriously about belief is considered dangerous. To be sure, thoughtful questioning of beliefs has shaken the foundations of more than one person's life. Such intellectual activity will continue to be "disturbing," but that ought not to be considered unfortunate. In our own day, for example, we cannot ignore the implications of the fact that our Judeo-Christian tradition has been male-oriented. We need to question the assumptions which value such beliefs. But if God can no longer be thought of only as "father" or referred to only as "he," what is to become of the beliefs of our ancestors? That question ought not to frighten us.

Those people who understand believing as a basic function of human reason and imagination, and beliefs as positions arrived at as a result of logical rational reflection upon experience, are in for trouble in a culture dominated by the more irresponsible forms of pietism.

Atheism

Pietism may be convinced that thoughtful belief is dangerous, but atheism is convinced that all religious believing is both useless and meaningless. Most atheists hold that religious beliefs are simply vestiges of an earlier stage of human culture from which we need to free ourselves. Thoughtful disbelief, while always present in history, is becoming increasingly common and accepted. There are many possible explanations for the increase in disbelief. Some people who hold a position of disbelief have quite correctly observed that religion is sometimes used by neurotic people to meet unhealthy psychological needs. Others have observed how religion has been used as a means of enslaving or oppressing people. For others, the persistent and ever present problem of evil cancels out all possibility of having religious convictions. And for still others, the concerns of religion remain unverifiable and, therefore, represent, at best, nonsense.

Those who hold these positions characteristic of reflective disbelief are often thoughtful, caring people who sometimes live lives committed to social justice and liberation. Who will deny that individuals and groups have been oppressed and their freedom denied in the name of religion? We must be sensitive to legitimate attacks upon inconsistencies and injustices perpetuated by particular religious beliefs. Religion *can be* more a symptom of neurosis than an expression of courage for the future. The problem of evil, the issue of verification, and the meaning of religious language are legitimate concerns, which no appeal to subjective feelings of a divine presence or call can avoid.

There was a day when such convictions and questions might have been easily dismissed or ignored. But with so many people openly professing thoughtful disbelief, they must be acknowledged and dealt with seriously. In any case, these disbelievers represent one more mounting challenge to the reasonableness of believing and belief in our day.

Believing may indeed be different in our day. Our beliefs may have to be expressed quite differently from those of our ancestors. But if we are to examine our beliefs and join the world in an exploration of believing, the best place to begin is not at the level of *what* we believe but in *how* we arrive at belief. And that takes us into the strange world of religious knowing.

· 3 ·

The Strange World
of Religious Knowing

What is the nature of religious knowing? It would seem that believers who start out by suggesting that they have a direct, simple knowledge of God derived literally from the Bible are in trouble from the start. Their argument will "die the death of a thousand qualifications." The Bible contains many apparent contradictions. Since all our understanding is human and therefore fallible, we really do not have available to us the infallible truth of God. God is not, even in Jesus, an *object* of our experience like the desk on which we write or the spouse to whom we are joined. We can claim that God lies behind our human experience, but we cannot prove it by any contemporary criteria of proof.

Of course the issue of religious knowing is not new. In the nineteenth century a debate raged in the Church of England. There were two sides: those who asserted that we cannot be conscious of the infinite, that is, God cannot be an object of our experience, and those who affirmed that we can have an objective and direct knowledge of God through revelation. While each remained convinced of their stand, it is important to note that the latter group was never able to point to any particular knowledge—the language of Scripture (Hebrew, Aramaic, or Greek), the Apostles' and Nicene creeds, the statements of the Ecumenical Councils—that was not the product of a human effort to understand the experience of God.

It appears that we cannot know God directly, no matter how much we wish otherwise. All that we can say for sure is that we are conscious of the limits of our powers of thought. And therefore we know that the possibility or impossibility of conceiving the infinite or transcendent has little to do with whether or not it exists.

Ways of Knowing

Essentially, human beings are creatures who have the power to experience *meaning*. We can never be content with biological satisfactions. We are forever disturbed by needs that are alien to animal existence. Our real longing is for meaning, and, whether we recognize it or not, all our strivings, whatever their apparent object, are directed toward the enlargement and deepening of this meaning.

C. G. Jung, the Swiss psychiatrist and founder of analytical psychology, described in his autobiography the catalytic event which started him on his lifelong quest for the collective unconscious—a common memory shared by all humans. He had been visiting daily, and for some time, a catatonic patient in the hospital in which he worked, when finally the patient broke weeks of absolute silence in this manner. He took Jung to the window of his room and called his attention to the sun and its rays, as they descended to the earth. Those rays, he said to Jung, are "the penis of the sun." Jung thought little more of it until he was in the national library of France, examining photographs of Egyptian tomb carvings. He came to a picture of the sun and its rays. The hieroglyphics that were also carved in the stone were translated beneath the picture: "Behold the penis of the sun." Jung was puzzled by this seeming coincidence of symbols. He had to know what it meant!

Religion is concerned with ultimate meanings. It seeks to integrate all realms of meaning from the standpoint of the whole—the transcendent dimension of our experience. But haunting questions remain in the realm of religious meanings: what is it to know and *how* do we know? Most of us have some thoughts about knowing in the realms of mathematics, the physical, natural, and social sciences, in philosophy, history, and the arts. But what about knowing in religion—a problem complicated by living in the twentieth-century United States, a pluralistic, religiously neutral, materialistic, technocratic, and, it would seem, pietistic nation? Perhaps conversion of one sort or another is necessary for religious seeing and hearing.

Of course, the word conversion conjures up for North Americans images of the strongly emotional nineteenth-century camp meetings or revival meetings and those traditions—Baptist, Methodist, Pentecostal—which made the sort of conversion experience that took place in those meetings an important part of their theology. While not excluding all aspects of this evangelical tradition, it would seem that there is a much more profound understanding of conversion as a way of knowing what needs to be explored. Historically, people have witnessed to conversions as dramatic emotional moments, but more traditionally they have described them as lifelong processes of the mind and heart.

If we use the common biblical image of God as the lover and we humans as the beloved, then conversion might best be understood as a divine courtship. There is a risk, of course, in using even this image, because our culture thinks of love almost exclusively as an emotion, and an overtly sexual one at that. But love is not just an emotion or a warm feeling. It is a power whose presence can be known in the entire person: mind, will, body, and emotions. It is an illumination that subverts any previous assumptions about what is real. This does not necessarily leave us with a cozy, warm feeling. Quite the opposite, it may demand of us a new courage. The great Christian mystics speak of the love which "inflames" us. To know the love of God is to know nothing more than that our passion for God is not in vain and we shall one day be united. Our memories are cleansed; our desire made whole.

Perhaps we can best illustrate our understanding of the character and importance of conversion in this way. A priest was studying for his doctorate at Marquette, a Jesuit university, where the teaching of the eminent Roman Catholic scholar, Bernard J. Lonergan, S. J., was dominant. Lonergan is perhaps the most distinguished living exponent of a historically rigorous, intellectual, theological methodology. His books are very difficult, closely reasoned, and, for some people, utterly convincing.

On this occasion the priest, a student of Lonergan's method, was entertaining Wolhart Pannenberg, an equally eminent Protestant systematic theologian, who teaches at the University of Munich. "Who is your principal mentor?" asked Pannenberg. Proudly the priest responded, "Lonergan." "What a pity," Pannenberg remarked, "he is nothing but a pietist!" Now a pietist, in these academic circles, is a person who is strong on emotion if not downright anti-intellectual. Since this is the last charge one could legitimately make against Lonergan, what did Pannenberg mean by this "put down" and why did he say it?

Lonergan's theological method, as rigorous as it is, holds that before one can move from the beliefs of others, from the tradition of the church, to construct a theology for oneself, there has to be *conversion*. Conversion for Lonergan is a falling in love and a subsequent opening of the eyes and ears to that which lies beyond the boundaries of our knowing. Pannenberg is committed, on the other hand, to the grounding of faith in reason alone and is opposed to any appeal to conversion. Conversion is to him a capitulation to feeling, and hence pietism. This does not mean that Pannenberg believes we can "prove" the existence of God, but he does hold that theological inquiry does not require conversion.

A good case can be made to prove that Pannenberg is wrong. We humans are whole persons, feeling and thinking. Our human nature cannot be divided. Conversion is a necessary part of the process of religious knowing, without which people will settle for a knowledge that lies only within the limits of their so-called objective experience, thereby isolating the intellect from the intuition. The new perception that comes with conversion, be it a matter of many years or a few seconds, is a gift in response to love.

It would seem that conversion is an essential way of knowing within the realm of religious meaning. Many people have lost sight of the transcendent in their midst; they have ruled it out or taken it for granted. What is needed, if we are "to know," is a lifetime of transforming experiences similar to one described in the life of Helen Keller, a woman who was both deaf and blind.

Helen Keller's breakthrough occurred on a hot summer day in Alabama when she first apprehended the meaning of a word and established a connection with the world and a possible means of relating to other human beings. At first glance there may appear to be no evident connection between us and Helen Keller. Her experience seems so unique that is has nothing to do with us who are not blind or deaf. Still the problem of religious knowing is that we do hear or see.

As a young child, Helen Keller was stricken by a disease which left her blind, deaf, and unable to speak. Until the age of seven she existed much like an animal in terms of her limited ability to communicate with other people and to understand the nature of the world around her. In the spring of 1887 her father employed a special teacher and companion for her, Anne Mansfield Sullivan. Working with Helen Keller through that first spring, Anne Sullivan taught Helen to spell rudimentary words by making certain finger signs on her palm. But this was a halting, inadequate form of communication. The child still responded much like a small animal in dealing with the people and things about her. All of this changed, however, one day in the summer of 1887. The record of that day was later made by Helen Keller herself in the following passage from her autobiography:

> We walked down the path to the well-house, attracted by the fragrance of the honeysuckle with which it was covered. Someone was drawing water and my teacher placed my hand under the spout. As the cool stream gushed over one hand she spelled into the other the word water, first slowly, then rapidly. I stood still, my whole attention fixed upon the motions of her fingers. Suddenly I felt a misty consciousness as of something forgotten—a thrill of returning thought; and somehow the mystery of language was revealed to me. I knew then that "w-a-t-e-r" meant the wonderful cool something that was flowing over my hand. That living word awakened my soul,

gave it light, hope, joy, set it free! There were barriers still, it is true, but barriers that could in time be swept away.

I left the well-house eager to learn. Everything had a name, and each name gave birth to a new thought. As we returned to the house every object which I touched seemed to quiver with life. That was because I saw everything with the strange, new sight that had come to me.

I learned a great many words that day. I do not remember what they all were; but I do know that mother, father, sister, teacher were among them—words that were to make the world blossom for me, "like Aaron's rod, with flowers." It would have been difficult to find a happier child than I was as I lay in my crib at the close of that eventful day and lived over the joys it had brought me, and for the first time I longed for a new day to come.

Helen Keller's experience is that of a second birth in the world. The word "water" had been lost; it was found; and in the recovery of this term, a term she had known before her illness, she was given a sense of life no longer constricted totally by the confines of her physical disabilities. While no sight or hearing returned, she began to discover a universe in which she had a place and a connection. The word gave her power to know beyond herself. It was a breakthrough, a moment of insight, a conversion. "That living word," she wrote, "awakened my soul, gave it light, hope, joy, set it free. There were still barriers, it is true, but barriers that could in time be swept away."

Knowing as Transformation

To know in the religious sense is to be open to transforming experiences. To understand what occurs during such transformations we will describe an account by a black American, Harvard-educated sociologist Bennetta Jules-Rosette, of her conversion to an African native church, the Church of John Maranke.

Belief, disbelief, and nonbelief are related to what people expect from their experience. One way of putting this is to say that we filter the data of our experience and identify what does come into our consciousness in terms of certain learned presuppositions. If we do not believe in God, it is because any data that might be interpreted to indicate the presence or the existence of an infinite being is either ignored (filtered out) or labeled without malicious intent to point to something else. This act is not a result of our conscious will; it is automatic. Inevitably, our reflection upon our experience has, as a precondition, certain primordial (elementary) images or symbols, learned from birth, which dictate the possibilities of what we perceive in our experience.

In her fieldwork as a sociologist, Dr. Jules-Rosette visited Zaire and Zambia and studied the Church of John Maranke, a local church grounded in the Judeo-Christian tradition and combined with an African religious idiom. It is standard for the study of any religion in sociology and anthropology to participate, observe, and record the ritual of that religion in minute detail. The effect of this experience on Dr. Jules-Rosette was to confront her images and symbols with alternative ones. This new set of images and symbols was assimilated into her consciousness, creating a conflict in her perception of the meaning and value of life. Here was a people whose expectation of life was very different from her own. Their expectations were grounded in a very powerful symbol system, which she perceived in their ritual. As she began to integrate their symbols, she experienced *an internal crisis in her life*, a disorientation.

It is possible, of course, to say that there was already discontent in her life. No one is completely free from internal disquiet and we are all susceptible to subtle urgings into new directions. Augustine of Hippo is a case in point. His awareness of conversion came only years after a restless search. The process is still the same, however. We are faced with conflicting symbols and a choice: flight or acceptance of one set or the other.

Dr. Jules-Rosette was led to accept the vision of the church of John Maranke and to begin the process of discarding those primordial images or symbols with which she came and of assimilating those of her new associates. We say "begin," because she testifies again and again to the fact that the choice to convert is only the beginning of the process by which one learns of a new reality. Conversion in one sense resolves the inner crisis, but only because it is a surrender to the possibility of a new awareness. It is the beginning of a long reorientation in a new understanding of reality. She lives now *as if* the God of John Maranke exists and has yet to know *what* that is or means.

The same process takes place in the writings of St. Augustine. If we examine his voluminous works, we notice that those composed closest to the time of his conversion are sharply Neo-Platonic, a philosophic tradition in which the pagan Augustine was educated. His later writings, however, while largely consistent with his earlier work, are far more pastoral and given to scriptural imagery.

The story of Carlos Castaneda, an American anthropologist, who over a period of approximately ten years became the disciple of a pagan Yaqui shaman in northwestern Mexico, is generally the same. He came to do research for a term paper and in the process of his investigation was confronted with a way of seeing the world which was utterly alien to his own. The symbols of the Yaqui shaman made their way into his consciousness and a conflict or disorientation ensued.

The shaman constantly attacked Castaneda's Western logic and told him that until he was released from his nurtured secular symbols he would not be able to entertain the possibility of another reality. The conversion was fulfilled when Castaneda symbolically threw aside all Western logic and hurled himself off a mountain into the abyss. Now his reorientation in the reality of his shaman master could proceed.

This pattern should be recognizable also in Paul of Tarsus. We meet him as Saul, the Pharisee, who went about " . . . breathing threats and murder against the disciples of the Lord. . . " (Acts 9:1). In the act of so zealously persecuting the church Saul is confronted by a symbolic language familiar yet very different from that taught him by the rabbis. There is a magnetic appeal in the quality of someone like

Stephen, whose martyrdom Saul witnessed, and other Christians, which must have made its impact upon him. It is easy to imagine the conflict that began to build in him, without his knowing it, only to be resolved in the drama of events recounted in Acts. Yet we know that event on the road to Damascus was only the beginning of his conversion. Paul speaks more of his own conversion as a process or reorientation.

The American social psychologist Milton Rokeach has for some years sought to understand the nature of values and the manner in which people acquire them. In his experiments he has discovered how it is possible to bring about a dramatic and lasting change in values by surfacing the value conflicts that people unconsciously hold. It would appear that we can profess opposing values—for example, forgiveness and strict punishment—without realizing it. The conflict remains suppressed. But when the awareness of such conflicts is made painfully unavoidable, it is our nature to make a choice between them. We become disciples. It is a movement from orientation, to disorientation, to reorientation.

Let us be very clear about this movement. As heirs of the American revivalist tradition, it is easy for Americans to think of conversion as the discovery of an assurance we did not have before. The opposite would seem to be the case. The orientation of the nonbeliever is far more likely to be that of assurance and comfort, even though it may be a peace obtained through tranquilization. The disorientation that characterizes the onset of conversion subverts all our assurance and calls us to a life of courage. Once again, it inverts our illusion of being in control and leads us to the edge of the abyss of the unknown and uncontrollable. Conversion is a passing over, in response to the touch of the other, to a new reality, which is frightening and uncertain. We do not believe that the truly converted have any sense of having "arrived," but only of having set out on weak knees and with a faint heart.

Ultimately religious knowing is different from other forms of knowing in that it requires what we have called *conver-*

sions as first steps in a lifelong process, a long search, carried out through the use of our intellects in a rational striving to make sense of our transforming experiences.

Blind Faith and Reason

Plato in one of his dialogues suggested that when people say "I know something"—for example, "I know that it rained last night"—they may mean to assert any one of three things: that what they claim to know is true—it really did rain; that they believe that it is true; or *something else*. The difference is between mere belief and belief based upon adequate evidence. There are many things we claim to believe but would not claim to know. When we claim to know something we generally mean that we have good reason for believing it. That is, we have adequate evidence. But we sometimes forget this when we deal with religious knowing.

There are people who might go so far as to say, "The Bible is the infallible word of God because this is what all right-living people have always believed." Such an emotional appeal to external authority stops all argument, even the possibility of convincing the antagonist of the truth of our statement. The antagonist can only go away angry at being accused of poor thinking. But it is not possible to defend your beliefs honestly and convincingly through an argument based solely upon subjective feelings. It is like arguing that chocolate ice cream is better than strawberry because "I like it better." Nor is it useful to appeal to an *external authority* without any willingness to subject one's belief to reasoned analysis.

Blind faith or *fideism*, as this is known technically, can be very obvious or very subtle. One example of "blind faith" is the person who argues that Jonah was literally swallowed by a "great fish" (Jonah 1:17). This story goes contrary to all we know about marine life in the Mediterranean. Even if we could imagine a fish large enough to swallow a person whole—no fish or ocean-going mammal of which we have knowledge anywhere in the ocean could do this—how could a person live without suffocating for three days inside a fish's gastrointestinal track? Some will answer, of course, that "the Bible says so" or "with God anything is possible." But to answer in this way is to violate all that we reasonably know to be true; we also miss the profound truth inherent in the story.

The story of Jonah is a legend, told to convey what its author believed to be a profound truth. To love freely and forgive is the most terrible of all pain, particularly when we are required to love and forgive the unlovable and unforgivable. The portion of the story which recounts the swallowing by the great fish both entertains and gives the occasion for the lovely poem that follows (Jonah 2:1–10): "Then Jonah prayed to the Lord his God from the belly of the fish, saying

> I called to the Lord, out of my distress,
>   and he answered me;
> out of the belly of Sheol I cried,
>   and thou didst hear my voice.
> For thou didst cast me into the deep,
>   into the heart of the seas,
>   and the flood was round about me,
> all thy waves and thy billows
>   passed over me.
> Then I said, 'I am cast out
>   from thy presence;
> how shall I again look
>   upon thy holy temple?'
> The waters closed in over me,
>   the deep was round about me;
> weeds were wrapped about my head
>   at the roots of the mountains.
> I went down to the land
>   whose bars closed upon me for ever;
> yet thou didst bring up my life from the Pit,
>   O Lord my God.
> When my soul fainted within me,
>   I remembered the Lord;
> and my prayer came to thee,
>   into thy holy temple.

Those who pay regard to vain idols
  forsake their true loyalty.
But I with the voice of thanksgiving
  will sacrifice to thee;
what I have vowed I will pay.
  Deliverance belongs to the Lord!

"And the Lord spoke to the fish, and it vomited out Jonah upon the dry land."

A more subtle example of irrational faith is found in the arguments that raged over the ordination of women to the priesthood and the episcopate before the General Convention of the Episcopal Church in 1976. One such argument was that it is impossible to think that it took 1,900 years for Jesus to make up his mind to ordain women, and therefore women should not be ordained. On the surface it looks like a good point. The authority to which this appeal is made, however, is to the inner thoughts of the Jesus of history. It is assumed these were an inherent part of the inner thoughts of God. It is further assumed that they included speculation on the doctrine of ministry. There are three assumptions here, which call for a reasoned analysis.

In reverse order, there is no record of Jesus "ordaining" anyone; not even St. Paul mentions the priesthood. Therefore it would seem reasonable that he had no doctrine of the Christian priesthood, which did not emerge until the third century. Obviously for Jesus "the priest" was the priest in the temple.

Furthermore, it is a matter of considerable debate whether Jesus' inner thoughts were the same as God's. Philippians 2:7 ([God] emptied himself, taking the form of a servant, being born in the likeness of men) among other places, would suggest they were not. It would violate the doctrine of the Incarnation.

Finally, it is impossible to know the inner thoughts of a contemporary intimate friend with completeness and absolute certainty, much less those of someone of whom we have no records written less than thirty-five years after his death two thousand years ago. (The earliest Gospel is Mark which is generally assumed to have been written about A.D. 65.)

What we have here is "blind faith" or an appeal to an authority, in this case the supposed inner thoughts of the historical Jesus—a claim clearly unexamined by reason.

Fideism, or blind, irrational faith, was condemned at the first Vatican Council (1869–70) but it goes much further back than that in Christian thought. The denial of reason and the equation of sentiment and truth are found in the second century. It appears to have always been a plague in the Christian community.

Fideism is a false answer, either conscious or unknowing, to the relationship between reason and faith. It pursues faith alone and denies the value of reason to be of any assistance in the knowledge of God. Aside from making any kind of discussion about the object of religious knowing impossible, except for those who share beliefs, it is contrary to the manner in which a thinking person comes to know anything. Augustine once observed, "Nobody believes anything, if he previously does not *think* it must be believed." We would qualify this by saying that nobody believes anything, *who does not have some overwhelming need to believe*, if he previously does not think it must be believed. The key word is *think*. At best we humans do not believe what does not appear reasonable, which is different from saying we do not believe what cannot be arrived at as a result of reason.

For example, there is a "Flat Earth Society"; it is a matter of faith alone which causes the members to believe that the earth is indeed flat. Most of us, however, believe the earth is round, because this is consistent with what our reason tells us. The religious establishment of Galileo's day suffered from fideism.

Fideism is wrong in its exclusion of reason, *not* in its insistence that faith is an essential part of religious knowing. The great sixteenth-century Anglican divine, Richard Hooker, taught that the authority of the church was like a three-legged stool, the legs being Scripture, tradition, *and reason*. Remove one leg and the stool topples over.

Conversion is a part of faith, which opens us to God. But for many of us, what we can finally believe is related to what appears reasonable. Some might protest that religious beliefs were learned from our parents and have never been questioned. Perhaps this is true, but the acceptance of such authority does not have to be unreasonable. It is more likely that the witness of our parents is something that through the years we have found *reasonable* to trust. The process of knowing always involves the acceptance of authority. If it were not so, we would have to "invent the wheel" again in every generation. But responsible knowing in all spheres of learning requires that we *test* that authority.

For example, adolescence is intended to be a time of such testing. Parents might say to their children: If you drink too much, you are going to be sick. The children are not sure of this, so they put it to the test and to their dismay and considerable discomfort discover its truth. Parents have also said that if they fail to study they will flunk out of school. It is just possible that the children, recalling that their parents were reliable in the first instance, consider that there is reason to accept their judgment in the latter instance. This is what is meant by testing authority and finding it a reasonable witness. We have to do it over and over again.

What has happened in this act of testing is that we have found the statement of the authority correlates with the data of our experience. This is what we mean when we say something is reasonable: what is said about experience "tests out." The process of religious knowing needs to test out. What has been said about God—found in our Christian texts (the Bible, various liturgies, the creeds, dogmatic statements of the church)—not only needs to be plausible, but should clarify and illuminate our common human experience. If we are not willing to test them out, this indicates that we are afraid they are false.

For example, there were two schools of thought in the Old Testament about moral responsibility: one which said the individual alone is responsible for his sins and another which said we have to take responsibility for what our ancestors did. It would seem that Deuteronomy is right, inasmuch as it is corrective on the Chronicles, Jeremiah, and Ezekiel. Certainly we have to take responsibility for our own sins, but scarcely a day goes by that we are not aware of being responsible for what our parents did and their parents before them. We cannot wash our hands, for example, of almost four hundred years of oppression of blacks because we keep no slaves and we do not practice discrimination.

So tradition (the Christian texts) must be taken seriously by the believer, but not as an arbitrary authority, untempered by the reasoned correlation of the intention of those texts to the data of common experience. This relation of text to experience means we seek to do two things. We try to identify and understand the central message of the texts and we strive to know in some clear fashion what is happening in our lives. Both of these things require disciplined thought. Then we bring together in reasonable fashion our understanding of the text's central message and what is happening in our life so that the former informs the latter in a meaningful way. We would not attempt to do this, obviously, if we had not already presumed in some sense the truth of the texts; at the same time, we are willing both to test that truth and to let our contemporary experience shape the form that truth takes in our lives. This is what we mean by choosing a faith informed by reason.

Perhaps an illustration is in order. Take the issue of abortion. A woman who is pregnant contracts German measles in the first three months of her pregnancy. Medical science tells us that in such a case she has a high probability of giving birth to a deformed child. Shall she seek an abortion? The Christian texts appear, at least on the surface, to speak clearly. You shall not commit murder (Deut. 5:17). Traditionally, moral theology has taught that to take another life without grave cause (self-defense, a just war) is a mortal sin. Yet we live in a vastly more complicated world than we did 2,500 years ago, or even 250 years ago. We can ask, "What is life?" Is it the same thing, necessarily, as the animation of an organism in a symbiotic relationship to either another organism (as in pregnancy) or man-made machinery (as in a respirator)? The Christian tradition seems often to have based ethical decisions on a certain "vitalism," which is the theory that to let nature take its course is generally correct.

Can we say this in the light of our new knowledge of how life itself comes to be? Does not the suffering of the mother challenge the presuppositions of vitalism and require that we look again at the Christian texts in a different light? It seems that Jesus' commandment to love God and neighbor above all else—and with our minds—as well as to be merciful, qualifies in some sense what before may have seemed obvious, if not easy. At the same time, we cannot dismiss this incipient human personality as simply a bit of tissue, a part of a woman's body, over which she has the final say. The texts do not justify any claim that we "own" our bodies in that way.

So we struggle between the preserving of life and bringing a deformed child into the world and the taking of a human life, and each in its own way, the texts and the experience, inform each other. The hope is that as we reflect on this struggle, an internally coherent meaning within the texts will emerge, which we can relate meaningfully to life as this woman lives it. If this happens, then we may make a judgment as to what is a faithful act.

Thus it is that we struggle to know, through the transformations of our past perceptions and the rational striving to make sense of our experience in the light of the experiences of others. The world of religious knowing is a strange world, but it is at the heart of our continuing human quest for truth.

· 4 ·

To Search for Truth

Without meaning, life ceases to exist. But without claims of truth, life is unbearable. To say that something is meaningful is to describe how it has helped us understand our lives; to say something is true is to claim that it reveals to us the very ground in which our lives are rooted. A claim of truth reveals our confidence in the process of living. Life, we seek to say, is not only understandable, life is worth living—life is trustworthy and purposeful.

It is one thing to say, "I get a great deal out of reading Genesis," but it is a different kind of thing for a person to say, "It tells me what God is like." Nonbelievers or even disbelievers can honestly say the former. It does not make liars out of them, because it does not require that they affirm any truth about what they have read. There is a clear difference between saying something is meaningful and that it embodies ultimate truth. For example, we have read the *Communist Manifesto* and found it meaningful, even though we do not affirm it as true.

However, as important as truth is, we need to be hesitant when speaking about it. It is easy to deceive ourselves into thinking because something is meaningful to us, it is also true. In moving from the meaningful to the true, we jump from a statement of "how it appears to us"—limited by our human experience and ability to find adequate descriptive words—to an affirmation of the nature of being itself, which has no limits and is beyond adequate description. This act of

affirmation requires the utmost humility. Indeed, it may well
be truly presumptuous to attempt it at all.

Humans can know directly only what is available to them
in terms of external appearance. Humans cannot know directly a thing-as-it-is. One cannot know the *being* of an object. It is possible to know a pine tree that grows on our
property, but we cannot know its treehood. Similarly, humans have no direct access to being itself, to God. The gap
between what things appear to be and what ultimately is
(i.e., God) is not simply a matter of degree; it is a matter of
kind.

Therefore, the truth of God cannot be described directly. It
has to be mediated through concrete manifestations—
actions, persons, symbols, and language.

The Problem of Language

Humans are the language they speak. There is an essential
relationship between humans and the spoken word. Without
words humans can have sexual intercourse, reproduce, defend themselves, build houses, find food, and eat. But without words people cannot think. What is more, without words
humans cannot ask those ultimate questions that make them
human: Who am I? Who are you? Do I matter? What is the
world like? Is there meaning to life? An animal may know.
But only human beings know that they know. Only human
beings can ask the questions, much less attempt to answer
them. This is what makes us "human": the asking and an-
swering of questions such as, "Who are we?" On the other
hand, language also calls humans into being. We can only be
what we know, and we can only know what is spoken. We
are our language.

Language enables people to share present experience.
Language also makes possible the illumination and sharing
of the experiences of people in the past. Through clarifying
and sharing, language represents experience in ways that
make it possible for others to understand and appropriate
historical experience.

But there is no language without the recipient need to

interpret what that language means. The technical word for this necessary process or interpretation is *hermeneutics*. Hermeneutics comes from a Greek verb meaning "to translate," as in the case of a foreign language. In other words, it is the act of taking someone else's words and putting them into our own words so that they become meaningful to us.

The Greeks had a god whose name was drawn from this verb; he was called Hermes. Among other things, Hermes was the messenger from the gods to humans. His task was to put into the words of human beings the words of the gods. This is the task of hermeneutics or interpretation: to discern in language the message of God so that it is meaningful to us in our common experience.

To engage in this interpretive task it is important to understand how language embodies what we have called meaning. Language began, of course, with speech: combinations of sounds *signifying by common consensus* particular objects, feelings, relationships, ideas, and so forth. Language, before humans began to write, existed only in the memories of certain people. For example, the epics of the Greek poet Homer were for centuries memorized and told. Only later were they written down. When writing was developed language achieved a life of its own. But it was and is still subject to common understandings. For example, Americans who visit England and English people who visit America are always astounded to discover what a different way each has with their common or shared language. "Lorry" doesn't sound much like "truck," nor does "wrench" bear much relation to "spanner."

Clearly language *represents* something else, for example, an experience. Sometimes language represents that which is clear and precise. We then know what the language refers to and we understand what is intended without any question. For example, if a person says, "I was in Chicago, Illinois, last Tuesday," we know what is meant. We may not find it very meaningful, but at least we are conscious that the speaker was seven days ago, for an interval of twenty-four hours, physically located in an identifiable piece of geography at the southern end of Lake Michigan and in the northern part of a state called Illinois. This kind of representation might be called a *sign*.

Sign language has definite limitations. If you are driving and see a sign saying, "CHICAGO, 10 miles," you know that you are near Chicago, but the sign will not help to get you there. It will not help you drive the car. After ten miles you may see a sign announcing, "CHICAGO," but it is still only a sign. It is not Chicago.

Sometimes language needs to represent that which does not possess the clear precision that signs do. We may not know what the language refers to: Or we may not be clear at all about what referent the representation embodies. Our language, then, is ambiguous. There is a *revealed-yet-concealed* quality to what is communicated. As a result, the question arises: "What does it mean?" Take this stanza from a poem by Gerard Manley Hopkins called "Henry Purcell" as an example. We read:

Have fair fallen, O far, fair have fallen, so dear
To me, so arch-especial a spirit as heaves in Henry Purcell,
An age is now since passed, since parted; with the reversal
Of the outward sentence low lays him, listed to a heresy,
⠀⠀⠀here.

There is little that is self-evident in this poem, or at least we suspect that there is more to what is being said than the banal fact that someone named Henry Purcell died sometime in the past. The words of this poem, therefore, are *symbols*.

Symbols are more complicated than signs. A workable definition of a symbol is a representation that intends to communicate a hidden meaning. For example, in this stanza from "Henry Purcell," the author begins by paying a tribute to a distinguished English composer of the late seventeenth century. But the poet believed that behind every appearance lies the hiddenness of what makes that appearance what it is. By the play of sound and the combination of words the hearer (more than the reader) could be led to discover the inner being of the referent. We do this by use of symbols, since they have double meanings: the obvious and the not so obvious. Through this double meaning the symbol *opens* the receiver to the possibility of new and deeper understanding. Symbolism, therefore, communicates what sign language cannot.

There is a curious thing about symbols. Signs are arbitrary. They mean what they represent because by consensus a human community decides that is what they mean. "Chicago" means that metropolis in northern Illinois at the southern end of Lake Michigan because some people decided that is what they would call it. But symbols are never quite like that. They bear in some sense a natural relationship with what they represent aside from what "we" decide to attribute to them. We make signs; we discover symbols. Symbols have a character of similarity, that is, they have within them something of that which they represent.

It ought not to be a surprise, then, to acknowledge that language can mean *more* than what its speaker intends. That is, language has a significance of its own, independent of the person who produces it. This is why interpretation is more difficult than simply "getting back" to what the author "intended." In the act of speaking, symbols emerge which certainly point back to the speaker's inner thoughts—but also point to something more. For example, the meaning of Hopkins's poem is not just a matter of what Hopkins intended, but the meaning which opened up to us as we read his poem.

The world of "facts and nothing but the facts" assumes that methods of measurement evolved by the physical sciences can be applied to all human processes. That is why there is still a lingering belief that a dictionary definition is a satisfactory description of an idea or an experience. But the language of experience is not the language of classification.

A boy burning with ambition to become a jockey does not study a zoology textbook. He watches horses and listens to what is said by those who have spent their lives around horses; he rides horses, feeds horses, and cares for horses. He lives with passionate feelings toward them. He may never learn how many teeth a horse has or the length of a horse's intestine. He is more concerned with a feel for, a response to, a living animal. Not all the knowledge in the world about anatomy can teach him horse sense.

It is the same with poetry, dance, music, and art. Analysis is never in any sense a substitute for a work of art. The best analysis can do is to prepare us to enter the work of art more perceptively. There is no way we can completely "understand" a work of art. Understanding and critical judgment are admirable goals, but neither can take place until the work of art is experienced, and even then there will be much that can never be fully explained.

That is why the question *what* does—a poem, a painting, a dance, a composition—*mean* is so useless. A more useful way of asking the question is *how* does it mean? To answer the question "how" requires our participation and leaves open our conclusions. It is to live in the world of symbols and metaphors.

Some scholars divide what we are describing as symbols into metaphors and symbols, the former being verbal and the latter being objects or actions, such as the bread and wine in the Eucharist or the act of immersion in Baptism. For some people metaphors, because they are verbal, are more explicit than symbols, the latter hidden deeper in the twilight of our consciousness. While we acknowledge the value of these distinctions, for our purposes we are using the word symbol to cover all these possibilities.

Having made this clarification, an illustration follows of the fact that symbols can bear a meaning that the person who gave them birth may never have intended: In contemporary abstract art the meaning of the artist is clearly difficult to discern. (Actually in so-called "realistic" art it is also difficult to discern but we can be misled by its recognizable images. What under the sun did the painters who depicted Jesus as a rather effete Anglo-Saxon think they were doing? This sort of representation is, in a sense, more confusing than any of Kandinsky's abstractions.) Sometimes people are hesitant about responding to such art, even if they feel a power in it, because they fear they may not grasp what the artist intended and thereby reveal their ignorance or be untrue to the original intention. But the point is that the artist's meaning is, if not irrelevant, not the whole or even the primary value of the painting. The question for interpretation is: What does it mean to you? Does it open you to the multiple possibilities of life's meaning? Or are you freed to reflect on who you are in greater breadth or depth, irrespective of what the artist intends? For any work of art to come alive, there must be a collaboration between the reader, the viewer, the listener, and the work. The greater the collaboration, the greater the work.

This symbolic dimension of language is essential to the sharing of religious knowledge. Its very openness moves us toward greater meaning. Some language, computer language for example, strives for a precision by reducing the symbolic element as much as possible. But other language, especially religious language (just as meaningful in its own unique way), depends heavily upon a symbolic dimension.

One way of illustrating the possibilities of language is through contrasting two kinds of stories, what have been called "open" stories and "closed" stories. Here are two very familiar ones that appear side by side in the New Testament (Mt. 22:15—22). The first story is the story the Pharisees had in mind. The second is the story that Jesus had in mind.

Some religious leaders come to Jesus, wanting to trap him. In other words, they want to force him into a contradiction, a situation in which he cannot win. They say to him, "Teacher, you are an honest man and you tell us what is God's law. Tell us, does not the law say we should pay taxes to the Roman emperor?" The trap was this: if he said "Yes," he would turn those who opposed Roman rule in Judea against him. They believed the law of God opposed any tribute to the emperor. If he said "No," Jesus incurred the wrath of the Roman rulers and their supporters, who were more interested in the law of the Empire than God. It is one of those questions such as, "Have you stopped beating your wife?" There is no way out.

Jesus answers with what seems to be a "yes," but in such a way that various possibilities of meaning are open. He accomplishes this by playing on the *ambiguity of language*. He asks for a coin and he takes it and inquires, "Whose head and whose inscription appear here?" The answer is obvious: "The emperor's." "Then," says Jesus, "give to the emperor what is his; but remember also to give to God what is God's." Many a sermon has been preached on the story interpreting it in terms of Jesus instructing us to pay our taxes. But is that its meaning? Is Jesus really dividing the world between church and state, as in the medieval notion of the "two swords," or Martin Luther's concept of the "two kingdoms"? One may well say that there is nothing that does not also have the image of God upon it. If that is true, what does the story mean? At least the question is open.

For just as in the parables of Jesus, a simple story challenges our customary orientation to the world and awakens us to the mystery beyond the limits of what we can describe firsthand. Our common sense is called into question. Our world and its usual understandings are subverted. The words have a double meaning and their very ambiguity points for us to a reality that transcends our common understandings.

Intuition and Imagination

Neither people who read the Bible and profess to be changed, nor people who stumble into the liturgy of the church and come out with a newfound truth, are necessarily deluding themselves or engaging in wish fulfillment. It is entirely possible that they have been encountered by what is "more," in the language of Scripture or in the liturgy.

It is important then to avoid a simplistic notion of religious knowing as *either* purely objective or subjective. Religious knowing transcends both of these points of view. Religious knowing from an "objective" point of view emphasizes the revealed-yet-concealed character of experience. Religious knowing also affirms, from a "subjective" point of view, the unique way in which an inquirer engages in knowing.

When we look at the moon, what do we see? Before the first man landed on the moon, what did we see? We saw a ball, with a frontside and a backside. Actually the data of the backside was not "there," but we "saw" it just the same. We knew that the moon was a sphere. It was natural for us to *fill out* the object beyond what our sense-data literally provided.

This "filling out" perhaps can be better understood if we consider a piece of art. Good art is not primarily a "facsimile" of the data of our experience. Good art is an appeal from the imagination of the artist to the imagination of the viewer. The artist makes use of the way the eye is "tricked" to show us a new world of possibilities. By the combination of color and line, the artist suggests what he cannot show, calling upon the viewer to fill in the blanks as we will.

At the same time, there is no such thing as observation without presupposition. No one looks out at the world, collecting data, with an empty mind. The artist knows that when we examine a painting we bring with us all kinds of theories about what reality is. True observation implies the asking of a question. But, typically, most people have a theory about the answer before they ever ask. Good art, by its arrangement of line and color (be it "abstract" or "representational" art), seeks to challenge whatever theory we bring with us, and thereby enable us, to discover reality afresh. It does this by suggesting *another* way of filling out the data of our experience. This is to say, the piece of art aims to appeal to our imaginations or intuition.

When early human beings looked out at their world they saw a subject *behind the object*. They spoke of this subject as the spirit-of-the-thing. Many modern people have been brought up to think that it is childish to put a spirit in each tree, brook, rock, and mountain, not to mention each person. For our ancient ancestors, a spirit inhabited all of life; within a person it was referred to as the "soul." Later, philosophers, scientists, and skeptics tried to change our minds by painting a different picture, a picture in which reality was nothing more than what one could see. That is, they projected an understanding of reality in which there was no subject behind the object, only the object itself.

This secular picture is open to question for many reasons and on many levels. But it is especially questionable because it neglects to take into account the fact that there is no such thing as *literal representation.* That is why the arts are so important to religion.

Religious knowing inevitably requires intuition or imagination. This is an essential, critical dimension of any act of interpretation—not just of the arts. It is the act of suspending judgment as to "what is," and playing the game of "what if?" Surely all of us remember doing this as children. "What if we play you are the Mommy and I am the Daddy?" It is only if we take ourselves overseriously as "adults," and forget the child that is in us, that we neglect the richness of playing "what if?"

It took a game of "what if" by those few brave persons that made up the first church to know Jesus as Lord. There was no name tag on Jesus saying: "Jesus, the Christ"! He did not fulfill the expectations for the Messiah held by the religious thinkers of his time or even the common people. He did not claim to be the Messiah. He appeared to be a peasant who spoke the rude dialect of Galilee. Most people saw him as just that and more—a dangerous blasphemer or disturber of the peace. What was required of Peter, Mary Magdalene, John, and the others to *see* in Jesus the Christ, the Messiah? At least, they had to be willing to ask themselves, "What if this *is* the promised one?" and then be willing to test that possibility.

Did you ever wonder why some people saw Jesus' actions as miracles and were impressed by them while others did not see these miracles and therefore dismissed them? Why was it that he was seen by some as the risen Lord and not by others? The Gospel itself tells us. It contrasts becoming as a little child—open-minded—as a necessary condition for coming to the Kingdom of Heaven (Mk. 10:15) with those who have hardened hearts, which is the same as a closed mind (Mk. 6:52). The childlike, open person, it would seem, can play at "what if" and the closed mind is only interested in the "what is."

This all says something about the nature of imagination or intuition. In the act of filling out the sense-data of experience, intuitive people are willing to experiment. Such people refuse to assume that "this is the way it has always been and therefore this is how it must be." The phrase "it has always been" goes no deeper than the presuppositions of the society in which one was brought up. There are countless presuppositions about the church. "The church service must begin with the vested choir entering led by the crucifer. It's always been this way." The custom is no more than a hundred years old. "Priests should wear a clerical collar and must not 'moonlight.' It's always been that way." Peculiar garb for priests dates from no earlier than the beginning of the nineteenth century, and prior to that clerical "moonlighting" was expected. The intuitive person is not bound by "it has always been," but is able to associate freely in order to ascertain better what lies *behind* the data.

Why did some people like Peter, James, and John leave their way of life to follow Jesus? It had to do with hope and a compelling desire for a better life. But it also required the willingness to play with the symbolic character of life. The power of Jesus was that he never fit the categories those around tried to impose upon him, including their understanding of the Messiah. Jesus was, in one sense, a primal symbol. For those with eyes to see and ears to hear—that is, with a keen, intuitive sense—the symbolic power of Jesus was just what their hopes and dreams anticipated. Jesus was God-and-Man; his well-known and acknowledged humanity became a metaphor for his hidden divinity. Those with open minds perceived in the peasant from Galilee that which was hidden—what the Bible calls the "glory" (Jn. 1:14, 2:11, 12:41).

Intuition is a necessary prelude to making critical judgments. Symbols lead to thought or the formation of concepts. If we ask ourselves, "What if?" the next question is: "Is it true?" This is a question requiring judgment. We know what is true by critically examining the possibilities presented by "what ifs" and judging which one does, in fact, fulfill all the data of our experience. "What if we play . . . ?" We must try to be true to the role as far as our intuition allows. It works for "what if we play Mommy and Daddy?" in much the same way as it does for an actor asking the "what if" as he studies the role of Hamlet. This is a critical action, which is rooted in our intuitive capacity. It is a fulfillment of a demand placed on everyone who truly wishes to know, to move beyond where they are, to become more. Such a movement demands of us that we be attentive, intelligent, reasonable, responsible, grow and, if necessary, change.

Without this responsible use of intuition, knowledge would never grow. The solar system was not discovered because a full-blown theory was uncovered in some obscure book from the past. The electric light was not discovered because a mathematician deduced it from an algebraic equation. Anesthesia is not the result of a syllogism. We all have access at this time to a conceptual theory explaining the solar system, the electric light, and anesthesia. But first there came the hunches of Copernicus, Edison, and Morton. The process of knowing demands that intuitive grasp, that willingness to risk the hunch as we look into the infinite unknown. Without it, knowledge would never be—nor would it grow. Einstein had the hunch; others worked out the prosaic mathematical equations which made the world accept the hunch.

The growth, this expanding horizon of awareness upon which intuition is based, is common to us all. There is always more to know—*infinitely more.* There is no reason in any authentic field of learning to think there will be a time when humans will know all there is to know about it. Quite the contrary. It seems that the more we know, the more there is to be known, and so we are always on the road of knowing, a road that continues to stretch out into the mystery of the unknown.

In a sense all knowing is religious knowing, because it is inevitably oriented to some ultimate mystery that lies beyond our limits of what we know now. Everything we experience—not just the things labeled by society as "religious"—and everything we seek to know, suggest something more in the very act of knowing them. Suddenly we seem very small and human knowledge very weak. Still, aware of our limitations, we seek to express what it is we have experienced.

Great care, however, needs to be taken that we never claim too much. Human knowing is such that we cannot and ought not envision a limit to what can be known.

The problem, then, remains—how is one to build a bridge from the finite to the infinite? Or better, how is one to find truth? If we cannot build the bridge by which to reach God, then God has to build the bridge to reach us. It is the nature of humanity to be open to such a divine gift.

· 5 ·

Removing the Veil

When the word "revelation" is used in Christian circles people tend to think of the Bible and the creeds. But the texts of the Bible and the creeds are historical documents. Every image in the Scriptures reveals the culture in which it was born. The languages of the Bible itself—Hebrew, Aramaic, and Greek—were products of particular peoples at particular times. The literary forms of the Old and New Testaments represent common ways of speaking among peoples long dead. The great dogmatic statements of the Ecumenical Councils in the fourth and fifth centuries are framed in the language of the period's prevailing philosophy. The later translations of the Scriptures and the creeds from their original languages are inevitably colored by the peculiar usage of language at any given time.

How can we equate such historical texts in any kind of one-for-one relationship with God? Any *equation* of an historical text, no matter how revered, with God and God's self-disclosure, is surely questionable. It is simply not useful or helpful to speak of the Bible or the creeds of the Ecumenical Councils as "revelation," much less our later translations of these documents, unless we keep always in mind that they are historical efforts, albeit inspired, to describe an infinitely more immediate revelation.

This is an important point which can profitably bear further illustration. If you keep a journal or diary, you undoubtedly describe in its pages your most intimate relationships, both with your inner self and with special people in

56

your life. The pages of such a journal *represent* your experience, but they can never be synonymous with that experience.

The Scriptures are, of course, similar to a journal or diary. If we understand this we can see how the author of the Fourth Gospel was speaking for all his fellow biblical authors and editors when he concluded with the words: "But there are also many other things which Jesus did; were every one of them to be written, I suppose that the world itself could not contain the books that would be written" (Jn. 21:25). If you have ever kept a journal, you will be able to appreciate his frustration. The same thing holds true for the church's dogmatic propositions.

The Council of Chalcedon (A.D. 451) declared that Jesus Christ is One Person in Two Natures, which Natures are united unconfusedly, unchangeably, indivisibly, and inseparably. It was a remarkable statement which is still authoritative today. But who would say that even this revered statement captures the experience of the living Christ?

Revelation is primarily an experience; only then, as a result of our need to express our experience so that it might be shared and recalled, do we attribute to it a certain objectivity.

Self-Disclosure and Relationship

The word revelation describes the experience of a veil being lifted or removed so that which was previously hidden might be made manifest. God does not reveal ideas about himself. God reveals himself. Through his actions, God communicates and relates. Revelation affects our consciousness and re-creates us. It transforms our relationships to self, neighbor, and the world. *Revelation is best understood as a personal encounter with a living, acting God.*

Revelation, therefore, is essentially a relationship with God, not a set of doctrines or new knowledge. For example, the Christian doctrine of eternal life is not essentially information about another world, but first and foremost the Word of God's presence in creating life out of death. Our lives can be shattered by sickness, failure, or accident. We are all vulnerable to forces beyond our control. Still the good news is that in every experience of death, God is present transforming it into life. For those who have experienced this revelation there is reason to reflect and express it theologically. But revelation, as a relational experience of God, is of primary importance.

If God is to be known to us, if we are to gain a true awareness or understanding of ultimate reality, it will be because that reality has in some sense been present to us.

Consider how two people become acquainted. Have you ever sat down in your seat on a plane and casually begun a conversation with the person seated next to you? If you discover mutual concerns the conversation quickens. Perhaps by the end of the flight you have become sufficiently interested in each other to keep in touch. Eventually, after numerous social encounters, you may become friends. And slowly, ever so slowly, you begin to know each other.

Notice that one person's knowledge of the other is not gained immediately. You become friends through a long process of mutual sharing and revealing. Only as a consequence of this interaction will you ever be able to say, "We know each other." Personal knowledge emerges in and through a history of mutual self-disclosure.

Revelation is neither an immediate insight or intuition nor a product of mere observation and inference. Revelation comes through a shared historical intimacy.

If I speak my mind to you, you can come to learn what I'm thinking; otherwise you can only conjecture it. Unless I choose to reveal to you the innermost secrets of my heart, it is unlikely that you will ever guess them. We come to know another as one we can love and trust primarily through words and deeds which disclose his character. God as a moral and purposive subject is beyond our reach. But God can be known, at least in part, if God acts in ways we can grasp.

THE ANALOGY OF LOVE

One limited but helpful way to understand revelation is to suggest that it is analogous to love. Love requires that lovers disclose themselves to their beloved. This truth becomes best known to us in a creative marriage. Whereas no spouse ever becomes totally transparent to the other, love demands that we share our inner self with the one we love. Sexual intercourse is a "sacrament" of this disclosure. There is nothing more beautiful than the love of a couple for whom sexual union is the symbol of their mutual self-disclosure. Such a bonding becomes the medium through which each realizes their being. We grow as we make ourselves utterly vulnerable to another. Our unveiling of ourselves, literally and symbolically, is an invitation for love. Our revealing solicits the discovery of the other self in us. To be is to be *in relationship*.

The Song of Songs (which is Solomon's) in the Old Testament is a hymn in praise of such love. The imagery is only very thinly veiled, if at all. Its understanding of love corresponds with what we have tried to express.

> [F]or lo, the winter is past,
> the rain is over and gone.
> The flowers appear on the earth,
> the time of singing has come,
> and the voice of the turtledove
> is heard in our land.
> The fig tree puts forth its figs,
> and the vines are in blossom;
> they give forth fragrance.
> Arise, my love, my fair one,
> and come away.
>
> (2:11–13)

> My beloved is mine and I am his,
> he pastures his flock among the lilies.
> Until the day breathes
> and the shadows flee,
> turn, my beloved, be like a gazelle,
> or a young stag upon rugged mountains.
>
> (2:16–17)

> What is your beloved more than another beloved,
> O fairest among women?

What is your beloved more than another beloved,
      that you thus adjure us?

                                          (5:9)

I come to my garden, my sister,
      my bride,
I gather my myrrh with my spice,
I eat my honeycomb with my
      honey,
I drink my wine with my milk.

                              (5:1)

I slept, but my heart was awake.
Hark! my beloved is knocking.
"Open to me, my sister, my love,
      my dove, my perfect one;
for my head is wet with dew,
      my locks with the drops of the night."
My beloved put his hand to the latch,
      and my heart was thrilled within me.
I arose to open to my beloved,
      and my hands dripped with myrrh,
my fingers with liquid myrrh,
      upon the handles of the bolt.
I opened to my beloved,
      but my beloved had turned and gone.
My soul failed me when he spoke.
I sought him, but found him not;
      I called him, but he gave no answer.

                                    (5:2, 4—6)

Make haste, my beloved,
      and be like a gazelle
or a young stag
      upon the mountains of spices.

                              (8:14)

  We cite the Song of Songs at some length because this
rather explicit description of love and love-making has been

used by Christian spiritual masters for two thousand years as the supreme scriptural account of God's self-disclosure to humans. It describes a quality of *relationship* which ultimately rests in mystery. For this reason, the mystery of love becomes a very powerful metaphor for the relationship between God and man.

It is no surprise that Revelation (21:1ff) describes the sanctified as the bride of the Lamb (i.e., Christ). It would seem likely that John the Divine was aware of the Song of Songs. A Jewish sixth-century Targum (a Targum is a loose translation of the Hebrew Scriptures into Aramaic, read until the tenth century in the synagogue after the reading in Hebrew) describes the bridegroom in the Song of Songs as Yahweh and the bride as Israel. Origen, one of the most distinguished of the early Church Fathers, explains that in the Song of Songs God is the lover. Sometimes he says that the church is the bride and sometimes that the individual believer is the bride. Gregory of Nyssa, another Church Father who lived a century after Origen, said that human perfection is the *process* of the beloved coming to know the lover; but that humanity never comprehends wholly the mystery of God's person. From the earliest centuries this sensual, passionate poem has provided us with an allegory to understand God's relationship to us.

What does this sexual image have to do with the subject of the chapter: revelation? The answer is "Everything!" For revelation is God's self-disclosure of himself to us as lovers reveal themselves to their beloved, or, as in the Song of Songs, as the bridegroom and bride disclose themselves to each other. It is deeply and intensely personal in that it is the gift of self in love, asking nothing but love in return. It is God's "emptying" of himself, as Paul says in Philippians (2:7): "he [Christ] emptied himself, taking a form of a slave" (translation ours).

Revelation is then God's invitation to us to come into being, not through words, but through the act of making love. God gives himself as a lover to the church, to each of us in the church and beyond, and as we are inflamed with God's love we come to know God and to be ourselves. To

know God is not to know about God as much as it is to know
God as in the Old Testament Adam *knew* Eve (Gen. 4:1, AV),
a synonym for sexual intercourse.

There is a difference between the knowledge of an object
and that of a subject. Pornography is about objects; sexuality
is about subjects. We can say we know *about* the battle of
Waterloo, the anatomy of the great white shark, the canons of
the Episcopal church, or the population of Kalamazoo,
Michigan. We can even say that we know *about* the president
of the United States or the queen of England, neither of
whom we have ever met. This is to know as to know an
object. Such knowledge is descriptive. We can know about
our car in that we can tell how much it weighs, how long it is,
how wide, and the horsepower of its engine. We can tell you
how much gas it uses. Our car is an object and nothing
more—even though in its recalcitrant moments we attribute
a certain perverse personality to it.

A person is never just an object. To know a person one has
to participate in that person's actions of thought, volition
(will), or feeling. Knowing what takes place between two
subjects (persons) requires that they share in the content of
the other's inner thoughts, that they live with them in their
decision-making, and that they feel with them. Without this
sort of intimacy we cannot know someone as another subject.

Imagine, if you will, a wife on the verge of divorce. We can
readily hear her saying to her estranged husband: "You do
not know me. You never have treated me as a person. You
have never asked what I think; you have never shared your
decisions with me; you are indifferent to what I feel." It
sounds like any number of movies, television shows, and
novels, does it not? What she is saying is that her husband
never attended to her actions in a way that indicated that he
cared what she thought, wanted, or felt. This is the difference between sensing a personal relationship and being
treated, in this case, as an object.

Of course, no two persons or subjects ever participate
completely in the other. We are embodied. We live in and are
aware of our *separate* bodies. The one thing we cannot share
with one another is what it is like to be *my* body. At the same

time, however, our bodies are the means by which we become aware of the actions of others and participate in their thinking, willing, and feeling. What makes the difference, in the final analysis, between our knowledge of someone whom we have never met and our knowledge of a loved one is that the latter is *present* to us.

If people choose not to reveal themselves and remain strangers they will forever remain inaccessible. Only specific acts on the part of another can unveil what is hidden. Revelation is a long process or series of events in which each revealing makes possible new revelations.

The Revelatory Event

We become "selves" in the process of social interaction and communication. Selfhood has a radical historical character. Our perceptions and conceptions are formed through historical events. Different moments in our lives, however, are of unequal importance. There are moments which shape our whole lives, as well as others of no lasting value. Our lives consist of certain turning points—moments of deep awareness—around which other events arrange themselves. In these moments filled with special meaning and their remembrances, our lives are shaped. The peak moments— these revelatory moments—tie together the loose ends of our lives; they give us fundamental orientation and meaning.

Such revelatory moments, we must understand, do not have to be times of sheer joy. The optimism of both humanistic psychology and—strange to say—certain Christian enthusiasts leads us sometimes to think they do. These revelatory moments can just as well be times of terror or tragedy as occasions of bliss or fulfillment. C. S. Lewis describes, in his autobiography, awakening to God's presence in moments of recurring joy. Yet another person, a person of great insight and depth, might become aware of God's presence with the tragic death of a close relative. The thing to remember is that a revelatory event is the cracking open of our secular world so that God's word may touch us.

Revelation means that part of our inner history which illumines the rest of it. Sometimes when we read a difficult book we come across a sentence from which we can make sense out of the whole. Revelation is like that. It is an intelligible historical event which makes all other events intelligible.

Revelation occurs through such events. Its content is not doctrine but story. Doctrine is the human attempt to explicate the story. As such, it is twice removed from the event itself. Revelation refers to that experience through which we discover ourselves in relation to the ultimately real, the norm by which all other reality is defined. We cannot understand revelation by studying the reports of others; it is always personal.

All revelation is from subject to subject, from divine subject to human subject. It is not information about God that God reveals. Revelation is the self-disclosure of God.

When Christians speak of revelation they point to history, to the life, death, and resurrection of Jesus Christ, but not as this can be known by external observations, but as it is remembered by participating selves. When we speak of revelation we mean that something has happened to us in our history which conditions all our thinking, and that through this happening we are enabled to apprehend who we are and that for which we are to live.

Revelation is not the communication of religious knowledge or the stimulation of religious emotion. It can be the occasion for the growth of knowledge and the experience of the holy, but revelation is the peculiar activity of God, the unveiling of that which is hidden. Revelation is the moment in our history through which we experience ourselves as known, in which we are surprised by the self-disclosure of light in our darkness.

A student once remarked, after hearing his college chaplain deliver a sermon, "You speak of praying to God, of revealing ourselves to God. But it is so one-sided. We speak to God and bare our hearts to God, but God never speaks to us; he makes no sign."

We often ask God for an unmistakable sign that he is there. But what sign would we accept? Some want miracles, and others arguments. Perhaps what we want is not what is offered. Perhaps our trouble is not that God does not reveal himself but that we do not see or hear.

Revelation means to disclose something that was formerly hidden. It does not mean, however, to discover. We discover something for ourselves, but we disclose something to another. Revelation implies the action of one person to unveil him- or herself and the action of the other to be open and accepting of that unveiling.

We mediate ourselves to each other through word and deed. And we construct an image of this other agent who, while transcending our direct perception, reveals to us his or her purposes and character.

Similarly God could hardly be known on the basis of our observations and experience. But God can be known if he acts to communicate himself in ways that enable us to construct representative images or symbols. We do just that through our myths and rituals.

Myths and Rituals

Our myths, and our rituals which symbolically reenact them, are expressions of the experience of revelation. They, in turn, open us to a personal experience of revelation. God does not become known in our myths and rituals, but they do frame for us a means whereby our awareness is deepened and broadened. As symbolic expressions of God's revelation to others they open us to our own unique experience of God's unveiling.

Generally myths indicate to the average person untrue stories (divorced from history) which attempt to explain life in some naive way. This seems incorrect. Myths do not describe something which is not so. They are rather the means by which we describe hidden truth.

A myth is a story by which a people chart its shared life and history. In all cultures people live by images. The meanings of things, our understandings of life and our lives are always best and most fundamentally communicated by word-pictures or myths. Our myths are pictures of reality.

We use word symbols in the same way that painters, composers, and dancers use their own symbols to share their experience of life and its meaning.

The Pawnee, a native American people, differentiated between true and false stories. True stories were about the sacred; false stories about the profane. True stories are myths; they point beyond mere history to the meaning of that history. Profane stories only recount historical events.

Sacred stories—myths—point to the transcendent in history. Their truth is found, not through logic or intellectual analysis, but through intuition. Myth unites history with the sacred, giving it particular symbolic significance in the lives of people. The story of the life, death, and resurrection of Jesus is, on the one hand, a profane, historical account, but it is also much more. It is a sacred story because it points beyond its historicity to the cosmic action of God in the salvation of the world.

Behind our myths lie certain primordial symbols related to death, birth, eating, sexual union, washing, separation, and so forth. These primordial symbols which lie behind our myths proclaim *a relationship desired but not yet attained.* We die that we might live; we eat that we might become what we are not yet; we make love that we might find love; we wash that we might be clean; and we acknowledge our separation that we might achieve oneness.

The primordial symbols, therefore, evoke the telling of a cosmic drama: the story of a love lost, a wandering in alienation and a recovery. All of this is the explanation of a moving drama which lies behind our everyday life and affects us at the deepest personal level. It is the story of our search for wholeness; our wish to be "somebody."

Being can, in the ultimate sense, come only from the source of all being—God. We tell the tale of our relationship to God in the hope that we might experience such a relationship. For when pressed to ask who we are and who we might be, we can only draw on primordial symbols and tell their story through myths enacted in ritual.

Ritual is the means by which people in community make

tangible in symbol, dramatic gesture, word, and song what they have come to believe is the hidden meaning of their experience in relation to the world, to others, and to God. That is why there have never been people without rituals. Humans are ritual-makers.

This innate need of the human being is early expressed in the child's ritual of bedtime. Certain toys must be in the tub. The order of drying and powdering the small body follows a regular ritual. Then come the prayers, the tucking in, the good-night kiss, the ritual of farewell for the night. Sleep tight. Don't let the bedbugs bite. God bless you. God be with you. See you in the morning. Good night. A ritual, even as simple a one as bedtime, is a collection of symbolic actions expressive of myths which undergird our lives.

Myth points to a condition of being that transcends our understanding of time. Therefore, the truth of a myth is not to be judged in terms of historical recollection or in comparison of intellectual proof. Myth is our only way of groping toward that truth which is beyond provable fact. Myth is the closest approximation to the truth of love available to us. One of the most extraordinary things about myth is that it makes known intuitively what it may take hundreds of years for the intellect to discover. The remarkable thing about the story of the Creation in Genesis is not how far it is from the facts as science now sees them, but how close it is. The ancient Hebrew poet saw the order of creation in the same way that scientists see the order of evolution.

The story of the Garden of Eden and Adam and Eve (Gen. 2:5, 3:24) is a nonhistorical myth. Nothing can be more beside the point than to go looking for the Garden in Iraq or Iran, its theoretical location. That does *not* mean what Genesis tells us about God, humanity, and their relationship is untrue.

Myth does not explain what we observe here on earth. It transports us from the illusions of a one-dimensional life and opens us to a universal history: God's saving purpose. There is no way that we can grasp God's vision for us except as a movement, a drama, conveyed to us in story form. The symbols of God's presence, God's grace, and God's love are woven into a finite, verbal picture, which refers beyond itself to the mystery of the experience of God.

Far from being a matter of only casual interest, myth lies at the center of human living and is of fundamental concern to anyone who takes life seriously. We ignore myth at our peril, because myth, along with ritual, constitutes that world of symbolic reality which opens onto the revelation of God.

· 6 ·

Sources of Illumination

Most arguments within the Christian community as to God's revealed purpose for humanity are made by appealing to tradition, but tradition is only one source of religious knowledge. Furthermore, the tradition of the community, if it is the sole source of making sense of the human experience of God, has a decisive shortcoming. It does not provide a common base of interpretation for the nonbeliever and disbeliever, as well as the believer—both in our pluralistic society and within each of us. If our goal is to transcend the division between private and public life and to form a consistent pattern of believing within all aspects of our person, then it is necessary to draw on a contemporary, common source of meaning. This means that we must look to the common life of late twentieth-century humanity.

We need to look at all dimensions of our shared human experience. Let us explore four contexts in which God's self-disclosure is a possibility in our contemporary world: the pursuit of knowledge according to the scientific method; the moral sense, or the perception of value; the feeling of condemnation and guilt; and the experience of suffering and death.

Scientific Method

Most of us are aware that for almost two centuries science and religion have been reputed to be locked in a struggle unto death, with science generally winning the battle. Typical of this contest was the debate between the evolutionists and the biblical literalists. From 1701 and on into our century, the Authorized Version of the Bible (the King James Bible) was published with marginal dates drawn from the biblical chronology of James Ussher (1581–1656), sometime archbishop of Dublin, a very learned man in his time. They began with creation in the year 4004 B.C. There have been Christians who have staked their very faith upon the truth of that date, while Charles Darwin and his followers have steadily accumulated evidence to suggest the world is about four and a half *billion* years old.

Such contests are fought on the wrong ground. Conclusions of this nature, be they scientific or theological, are only models of what may be—just as we may build a "model" airplane or ship, not facsimiles of them. There are no facsimiles in the human mind of being as it is. There are only models! It is futile, therefore, to draw up opposing "orthodoxies" and fight it out. To do so proves nothing. Undoubtedly Archbishop Ussher, in the light of evidence to which he never had access, was wrong. This does not mean that someone who claims that the earth is four and a half billion years old is necessarily right, or that to prove this contention refutes God as creator. It proves nothing whatsoever—except that human beings are prone to make mistakes.

When Galileo came out with his discoveries and horrified the church hierarchy, all that was being upset was a set of theories formulated by human beings. It did nothing whatsoever to affect the glory of God. We should never feel that we need to protect the faith from the discoveries of science. Science only shows us the greatness of the Creator and the extent of human fallibility.

The fact is that as scientists explore the universe in which we live they typically are confronted by an amazing revelation. Rather than "getting to the root of things," they find the universe ever more complex. In other words, the more science discovers, the more scientists become aware of what there is to know, which they do not know—increasing as in a geometric progression.

A clinical psychologist, a very competent professional, widely respected in his field, recently reported that he had just returned from a week's retreat at a Trappist monastery! And he had one important learning he wanted to share, namely, that he was becoming increasingly aware, as he studied and practiced psychology, that human beings are a mystery, never reducible to the models of Freud, Jung, transactional analysis, sociobiology, or any other school of thought.

Nuclear physics reveals a similar truth. The ancient world coined the word "atom" to indicate the indivisible, basic particle of which the universe is built. Most people are aware that this concept was appropriated in the development of atomic physics over the last several generations. Most of us are also aware that toward the end of the nineteenth century the atom itself was seen to be made up of various particles, beginning with the electron, and moving on to protons, neutrons, and so forth. The question of the basic building block of the universe was pushed that much further back. But the search continues and gets infinitely more complex.

Surely this is not to criticize those scientists who prematurely believed that they had "arrived" at the truth, nor are these accounts worth telling simply because they are fascinating. The point is that scientific models are efforts to give substance to what is ultimately a mystery: the infinite nature of the universe. Science has not grapsed this universe and, if we can judge from the evidence on all sides, never will. Yet science obviously presumes that the universe is just what the word means—a unified whole, which is intelligible. There is no way that anyone can "know" that there is a fundamental order to all we have experienced and will experience, an order which is accessible to human reason. It is an act of faith. And the true scientist makes much the same act of faith as the believer.

Albert Einstein wrote this in his Journal:

> "What is the meaning of human life, or, for that matter, the life of any creature? To know an answer to this question means to be religious. You ask: Does it make any sense, then, to pose

this question? I answer: The man who regards his own life and that of his fellow creatures as meaningless is not merely unhappy, but hardly fit for life.

And Einstein also wrote:

A scientist's religious feeling takes the form of a rapturous amazement at the harmony of natural law, which reveals an intelligence of such superiority that, compared with it, all the systematic thinking and acting of human beings is an utterly insignificant reflection. This feeling is the guiding principle of his life and work, insofar as he succeeds in keeping himself from the shackles of selfish desire. It is beyond question, closely akin to that which has possessed the religious geniuses of all ages.

Of course one must not jump from saying that "order" requires an "orderer." This is not the point. Cause and effect themselves have no validity outside of our own presuppositions about the nature of the world. The point is that scientific method is founded upon an expectancy similar to that held by those who in the first century looked for the Messiah, or Christian believers today who believe that Christ is present in their lives, giving them order. No one has ever seen God. But we all know, especially scientists, what it is to think in terms of what may reasonably be trusted to be true. Somehow we cannot help but have faith that it all makes sense.

It is interesting to note that the author of the Fourth Gospel identified Jesus Christ with an intelligibility that some ancient philosophers believed held the universe together, an intelligibility in which every human being partakes. He wrote, "When all things began, the Word already was," and goes on to tell us that "the Word became flesh" (Jn. 1:1, 14). The Word was the rational "glue" of all that is. Scientific method trusts in a similar rational "glue," a contention for which it, too, has only an intimation.

What does this do to the supposed life-death struggle between science and religion? One can only hope it makes it absurd. Both scientism—that brand of secularism which believes science will eventually have all the answers—and theological triumphalism—that brand of fundamentalism which believes the church or Bible has all the answers—must realize the ridiculousness of their positions.

Certainly God is not to be "found" simplistically in the laboratory. The sacred does not lie at the end of a telescope, a microscope, or a syllogism. But perhaps the trust of faith that God exists can be revealed in the world of science as well as within the tradition of the church.

We cited earlier the clinical psychologist whose science pushed him into an inner quest within a monastery. What was not said was that this was a psychologist who was reared in the Episcopal church, but now finds his parish secular and sterile. The reasons are, as he explains them, that his parish is self-serving, lives only for its own institutional life, and is basically committed to the legitimatization of secular ideals. Revelation for him and for many others is in the mystery that science must probe *with passion and with faith.*

Moral Value

There appears to be a "primordial moral experience" common to all people that illuminates our lives. We describe it as a sense of responsibility. That is, we have a sense of being answerable to an unconditioned claim on our human conscience. We do not even have to name this transcendent imperative. We feel its demand and our need to respond. This is our basic moral sense. As Bonaventure, the thirteenth-century Franciscan scholar wrote, "The notion of the highest good is necessarily imprinted in everyone who deliberates." We experience, reflect, decide, and act in a mysterious milieu of an unconditioned gift of love. It calls us to sacrifice our life for a cause we may never see fulfilled, to give unstintingly of our time and efforts to those whom we will never see, and to risk professional disgrace and social rejection in the name of what we think right and good.

Of course we are all familiar with looting in times of natural calamity such as earthquake, hurricane, or flood. It shocked many people to learn that bodies of air crash victims were looted before they could be removed from the field where they had plunged. Acts like these call up the horror of social chaos. Yet in the midst of such tragic events others of us are deeply offended, even as we are also caught up in the social collapse. We act with a courage that we probably never knew we had. There is more to our action than any positive reinforcement by the social environment can explain.

Moral outrage in the face of no reinforcement for ethical behavior is the result of a primordial experience of value which emerges in this way: First, there is the collapse of social norms. One can steal at will. Then there is a mounting sense of crisis. To steal violates the "order" of things. Third, there is an appeal to symbols of value independent of our own making. To be human is to honor those things that belong to others. And last, there is a reconstitution of the society in some form in which this value is given special prominence.

This process is not just known to "believers." It is common in the life of all people, even those who deny its truth. We do not believe that in the absence of positive institutional reinforcement for moral good we all revert to the amoral behavior of lesser animals. In fact, it would seem that within the context of such an experience one who is open to mystery can discern the completely undeserved gift of human life. We live not for ourselves but for the infinite other that surrounds and pervades our finite existence. To be aware of our human primordial moral experience is to have the meaning and purpose of life illumined.

Anxiety and Dread

A priest recalls the experience of counseling with an elderly woman who presented herself to him as needing forgiveness from a terrible sin long past in her life. The two of them, the priest and the elderly woman, went into the church for the Sacrament of Reconciliation and stayed there for an hour and a half while the woman spread out her grief. What was the sin? When she was ten years old her mother had given her a nickel to put into the alms plate at church. Instead of doing as she was told, she kept the nickel and spent it on candy. Such guilt, totally out of proportion to the offense, is neurotic. But not all guilt is neurotic.

In all serious illness the horizon of our world shrinks to the edge of our bed. We are cut off from the world of the healthy. Our alienation from the source of life impinges upon us. It seems at first strange, but then upon reflection it is understandable, that the sick person experiences in this state another sort of condemnation and guilt: anxiety and dread. The critically ill are paradigms of us all, since the only difference between us is their explicit awareness of mortality. If we reflect upon our finitude, as the ill inevitably do, we experience a sense of judgment. If we want to see someone with a terminal illness, we only need to look into the mirror. We are all born to die.

St. Paul, a man acutely sensitive to human alienation from the source of being, speaks for all people when he cries out, "Wretched man that I am! Who will deliver me from this body of death?" (Rom. 7:24). Of course, he answers himself, "God alone, through Jesus Christ our Lord!" But we err if we move to his conclusion without dwelling upon his despair or, as theologians and philosophers over the last hundred years or so have called it, anxiety or dread. This feeling is at the very root of our being and is not neurotic. It is the common experience of all perceptive persons: nonbelievers and disbelievers as well as believers.

The experience of dread is the awareness that, when "the chips are down," we are alone, without support. There are no arguments that can save us from the haunting fear that life is, in the final analysis, absurd. Is it the feeling of abandonment known even to Christ, when he cried from the cross, "My God, my God, why hast thou forsaken me?" (Mt. 27:46). We must not romanticize this despair. St. Paul means it when he says, "[You must] work out your own salvation in fear and trembling" (Phil. 2:12). The Danish theologian, Soren Kierkegaard, made much of Paul's words in claiming that our relation with God comes only in the midst of dread, in which we take an utterly unsupported "leap of faith."

Anxiety and dread are common to us all. Whether or not

we can leap into the unknown abyss, trusting in a God who appears to have utterly abandoned us and condemned us to an absurd end, is another question; Kierkegaard believed it is the only possibility for an authentic self. Thomas Merton, the contemporary spiritual master, said that dread was the necessary experience of those who contemplate God. In any case, it is in the midst of our common human experience of anxiety and dread that the meaning and purpose of life can be illuminated.

Suffering and Death

Clearly suffering and death are related to anxiety and dread, but there also can be an experience of revelation in suffering and death.

There has been in recent years a remarkable upsurge of interest in death. The study of the psychiatrist Elisabeth Kübler-Ross into the dynamics of dying has become widely known. She herself has, through her extensive research, come to the conclusion that there is life after death, based not upon a commitment to Christian witness so much as a recounting of the experiences of those who have clinically died and have been revived. She is not alone in her research or published conclusions.

The fascination of death is, of course, related to its absolute unknown quality. Our fear of it derives from our loss of control. It is not something we generally do to ourselves, but it is done to us without our consent. Society today has taken it even further out of our control. We no longer die at home, surrounded and supported by family and friends. We die in hospitals, often alone, in the company of respirators and I.V. tubes.

Karl Rahner, a contemporary theologian, has said that if you wish to picture human beings as they really are, you have to see them as they die. We are not secure on this earth and we are not yet aware of any life beyond, but we are suspended in between heaven and earth. Death is the final darkness, the barbed meaninglessness we must ultimately confront.

This kind of meditation does not sit well with contemporary people. We have hidden our dying in hospitals and covered over our suffering with pain-killers and tranquilizers.

But many doctors know that if they give a grieving person tranquilizers to help them through the first days or weeks, the grief which should have been experienced at that time will hit later and with far more brutality than if the normal grieving had been experienced at the appropriate time.

Suffering and death in their very uncontrollableness threaten our presumption that to live is to be in control. Much of our science since the eighteenth century has been devoted to enabling us to control our environment for the betterment of humanity. Suffering and death threaten all these attempts.

The result of our striving to control is that we have far less control over our environment than did our grandparents. The elevators which were to keep us from climbing stairs and which permitted skyscrapers frequently break down. When we travel we do not know whether or not our plane will be hijacked, or whether or not our car will be hit by a drunken driver. We know we have little control over the weather.

What kind of revelation can we hope will emerge from our awareness that we lack control over human life?

It is interesting that the problem of evil is particularly used by the disbeliever of our day to bolster the denial of God. If God is all-good and all-powerful, how can we explain the existence of undeserved suffering and death? The god of such a disbeliever is, of course, the god who controls. So the cross is as much an absurdity to such a disbeliever as it was to the ancient Greeks, for it suggests that God would permit his only son to suffer and die such a hideous death. He sees no reason why God just could not "fix it," if he were really the God we claim him to be, like "fixing a traffic ticket." If God is not such a God, the disbeliever would say, there is no God at all, by *definition*.

But it seems vital to challenge the idea of God as a kind of "cosmic fixer." Images of control and prediction are not essential to the experience of God. The possibility that our age is more one of unbelief than belief is not because we have discovered that God is an illusion resulting from some personal immaturity, or that God has "died." It may very well be the result of our insistence that unless God conforms to our values, which make control so very important, God is not "there," when in actuality he is very much "there." After all, some people denied God was in Christ because he did not do what was expected of him.

It is entirely possible that God is to be experienced in relation to us not as we "solve the problem of evil," but as we live into suffering and death. This is not to suggest that we seek them, but that we cultivate a very atypical style for contemporary people, an openness to the possibility of what we may know when suffering and death overwhelm us.

We are suggesting that the experience of God lies beyond our control in the uncertainty of death. If we are to know the encompassing God, we have to face the encompassing darkness of suffering and death. It is natural to acknowledge our dependence and fear of death. Jesus called God "Abba." It is usually translated "Father," but its actual connotation is much closer to "Daddy." It is the cry of children who awaken to find themselves in the dark and call out "Daddy" or "Mommy." We fear the uncontrollable, so we pray in our darkness not out of any constituted belief, but out of sheer fright—"Our Daddy, Our Mommy, in heaven . . . ."

It is impossible to be so wrapped up in the present that we are unaware of death. And we can never be so happy that we are oblivious to pain. Suffering and death constitute a common experience for us all, an experience for which secularism has no adequate language of explanation. It either hides from it or philosophizes about it, and neither really satisfies our human longing. For this reason it would seem that such a common experience may also offer the possibility of knowing God.

Here then are four examples in common experience, through which we might be found of God: scientific method, moral value, condemnation and guilt, and suffering and death. There is no intention to suggest that if one becomes aware of these aspects of experience that there will be an immediate awareness of God. No guarantees, only a possibility.

Illumined by Angels

Our sense of the intelligibility of the universe, our perception of moral value as given to us rather than engendered by us, our leap of faith in the midst of dread and our childlike cry in the face of uncontrollable death—none of these experiences in and of themselves "produce" God, much less a Christian understanding of God.

What is it that illumines such experience? What is the origin of the confrontation in revelation that illumines the experience and says this is of God? The Bible speaks of angels who point to our common experience and tell us that something very uncommon is happening, such as the birth of a baby to simple Galilean people in a cave outside Bethlehem (Lk. 2:8−14). The word "angel" means "messenger." Angels are messengers from God who point out to us the extraordinary dimension in our ordinary experience.

What confronts our human experience and says, "there is more to this than meets the eye" is our *memory*. Our individual and social memory is an angel. Memory, like angels, is a mystery. It is a mystery to the neurophysiologist who does brain research. Are images from the past, from humanity's primordial past, stored within the central nervous system? It is a mystery to the philosopher. Is there such a thing as mind apart from brain? A woman recalls her answer to this question when she was seventeen; it was after the death of her father. A young man insisted that her father could no longer *be*, because consciousness depends on the cerebral cortex. And she replied, "Because I am extremely myopic I depend on my glasses to see, but my glasses do not do the seeing; I do, through them. And our brains do not do the thinking; we do, through them." It was a fascinating reply. Of course, we do not understand the mystery of memory but we do know that it often confronts us in ways that raise questions about our experience and provide us with intimation of its possible meaningfulness, just as the angels in the Bible are said to have done.

The Greek word for truth is *a-letheia*. It means literally "unforgetting." To know means to remember. In Greek mythology the river Lethe ("forgetfulness") ran through the underworld. The souls of the dead drank from this river to forget their former lives. In Virgil's epic *The Aeneid* the souls of those waiting to be reborn wander along the banks drinking from the river Lethe so that in their new bodies they will have no memory of their previous existence. In Norse mythology the goddess of sensual love, Freyja, gives to her lover a drink of a memory-beer, that he might "unforget" his genealogy. It is the reverse of the river Lethe, but is constructed on the same intuition that memory is related to understanding.

People in Western civilization have tended to neglect the role of memory in understanding and have emphasized observation through the five senses. We need to once again consider that we always observe our experience as persons possessing memory. Our ability to learn from our experience depends directly on the richness of our conscious memory, just as the wheat harvest depends for its abundance on the richness of the soil. Our minds are never barren.

This thought seems to us particularly compelling when one realizes that stories lie at the heart of our awareness of God's presence in our lives. Storytellers rely heavily upon their memory. If we tell a story about a fourteen-year-old, we must remember what it is to be fourteen. But this is not a looking back; it is a bringing into the present. This is the meaning of the word "anemnesis." The Eucharist, for example, is a rite bearing the Church's memory of the Passion and Resurrection of Jesus. It is not an act of nostalgia. It is an act of anemnesis, making present.

Each of us has a memory, by which we mean the recollection of significant events that are ours alone. Erik Erikson suggests that the possibility of revelation is built upon the memory of our first year's experience with our mother. It is the time when we build through human interaction a sense of trust or distrust in the universe. We learn our religion at our mother's breast as well as at "her knee." Memory is not just the recollection of what we are told in words, but what we perceive in the facial expressions, the tone of voice, the movement, and the touch of those who are of significance to us.

Sometimes, of course, personal memories can be destructive. The beginning of psychotherapy is insight into these personal, negative memories. There is an approach to emotional and spiritual suffering which is called "the healing of memories." If our memories are all of distrust, pain, conflict, or of being ignored, then all of our experience will be seen in this light. If our experience is of faith, hope and love—the three virtues of which St. Paul speaks so movingly (I. Cor. 13:1–13)—then our experience may well be seen as revelatory.

But our picture is bigger. There is more and more evidence to indicate that one dimension of our memory is racial or social. By this we mean that humankind itself carries a common memory out of its evolution over the last million years or so. What we are beginning to learn is that there is some relation between our genetic inheritance and memory. It seems that the human race has a common memory passed on from generation to generation, a memory humans can actively draw upon in their pursuit of understanding their experiences today. Why is it that we find identical images representing similar experiences in cultures which have had no contact with each other? Any student of mythology or historian of religions is struck by the common bond that unites the symbolic reality of humanity.

The snake is an image of the feminine in Central America, southern Africa, the Middle East, the Far East, and in Christian biography of the saints. Why? For what reason did both the Mayans in Mexico and Guatemala and the ancient Egyptians build sacred structures in the form of pyramids? It is strange that the tree represents for so many unconnected cultures the union between heaven and earth, including some Christian homes today, where for reasons we have probably never contemplated we put a star on top of the

Christmas tree and artificial snow or grass at the base, suggesting the joining of heaven and earth. Coincidence?

Jung noted that in the fantasies and dreams of his patients the same images recurred again and again in people who had no demonstratable common link. Jung concluded that there is a shared objective psyche in all humans, a collective memory. It seems reasonable to assume that humankind possesses some kind of corporate memory, rooted in its very origins.

Of course there is something strange and even a little alarming about all this. An inherited racial memory which acts as an "angel" making it possible for us to see God's presence in what appear to be imaginary experiences is an odd thing to contemplate. Still, the contention that we are confronted by the hiddenness of our memories and that we have our common experiences illumined by our memories might be the clue to the human awareness of God.

The Tradition

But there is more, for everyone shares the conscious memory or tradition of some community. For Christians it is the Scriptures, creeds, liturgies, lives of the saints, and so forth. The Bible is the normative memory of the church, but the Bible must be seen in a proper perspective. It is a way of remembering, and it does belong to the church. With all the good that the invention of printing and the Protestant Reformation brought, they also obscured for many people the place of memory in our piety. The Bible to the ancient and medieval churchman was not so much a reference book to be used to prove the rightness of a position as it was a story book to be used to frame perceptions of life and to summon readers or listeners into an awareness of their experience. It is the difference between oral learning, which comes from hearing and remembering a story, and linear learning, which comes from reading and underlining a book. The former is more internalized, more a part of us.

There is much evidence to support the theory that a child's most formative years are over at seven. If children are properly brought up until they are seven nothing will change their basic orientation. The same would hold true if the child is brought up improperly. Perhaps this is a bit exaggerated, but the modern psychology of learning does point in this direction.

It is the primary task of all communities to build within the lives of children a conscious communal memory by literally engulfing them from an early age in the myths (stories) and rituals (liturgical life) which bear the community's tradition and inform and sustain their lives. Throughout our lives this conscious communal memory encounters our everyday experiences and provides us with the means by which they can be illumined, by which the meanings of our experience can be understood.

In our encounter with our community's conscious memory the awareness of our experience is given direction and we are granted a sense of meaning and purpose. This is why it is so important that our children know the stories of the Bible.

It has been suggested that the meaninglessness of life in contemporary America, its frequent banality, results from the sterility of conscious community memory. In placing our old people in "homes" we are banishing the riches of their memories. Whereas, in contrast to our "civilized" behavior, "primitive" people honor and revere the old members of the tribe because they are the keepers of the memory.

In Kurt Vonnegut, Jr.'s novel *The Sirens of Titan*, Malachi Constant is lured to Mars, having lost his father's money. He becomes Unk, a private in the Martian army. Like all Martian soldiers he has an antenna implanted in his brain, which brings unbearable pain every time he tries to remember anything. Life on Mars is utterly empty. Unk murders his own best friend without recognizing him. He cannot even recall a letter he wrote to himself before his memory was "cleared." While he still had memory, Unk was "courageous, watchful and secretly free." Now there is only meaningless violence. Thus it is that Vonnegut satirizes our society, a society where memory is so impoverished that we find great difficulty in trusting to much more than a mindless hedonism.

Secularism needs no antennae in the brains of its citizens.

Symbolic deprivation does just as well. Outside the private home there is very little that feeds the memory, and within it, unless we make a consistent effort, it easily falls away. The media (television, radio, newspapers, magazines) tell relatively few stories worth remembering and offer little food for meaning beyond violence and sensuality for their own sake. Somehow the quest for revelation involves the demand that we regain a conscious community memory. How can God disclose himself to a people who have no way to speak of his presence, who are culturally retarded? Even more, what is the possibility of our seeing God if our memories are barren?

Most people have had the experience of writing a letter to someone they love, or perhaps a poem or song, in which they have sought both to put into words the meaning of that love and, consequently, to identify the changes made in them by love. What an effort it takes! Most people are at a loss for images. When we read what we have written it makes our deepest feelings seem trivial. We may even be embarrassed. Few of us are a Robert Burns, a William Wordsworth, or an Emily Dickinson. Yet it is in reading great love letters and poems, or in hearing songs, that we learn to write of our own love and even to know that what is happening to us is love. So it is also true in speaking of God and knowing his presence among us. We must hear and read what the church has said before in its tradition in order to know more clearly how to express the experience of God and how to see him in our midst. The value of the tradition is that it illumines our life.

A Living Tradition

The memory of the tradition and its meaning for us has been an issue very much sharpened in recent years in the Episcopal church, as well as elsewhere, in regard to the ordination of women to the priesthood and episcopate and the revision of the liturgy, including new translations of the creeds. What is tradition? What is its claim on our present belief and practice? Sometimes theologians speak of Scripture *and* tradition. We are not making that distinction, as honored by time and theological discourse as it may be, but *include* the Bible in whatever we mean by tradition. Tradition is for our purpose here all authoritative meaning within the life of the Christian community.

Theologians who venture out on the lecture circuit know well the experience of being told that all their fine words are very well and good, but what people need is the "plain truth of the Bible" or the "clear teachings of the church." Frequently our critics will refer to Jude, who wrote about the faith which God entrusted to his people once and for all (Jude 3). The implication is that there is a core of tradition within the church which is clear and precise, whose meaning and subsequent demand upon our actions are always and inevitably fixed.

There is no doubt that there are traditions, by which we mean propositional statements, which have greater validity today than others. But none has an existence independent of present experience. For example, the tradition requiring circumcision was once debated in the apostolic church, with the decision, at the Council of Jerusalem, that this tradition was no longer binding upon Gentile converts to Christianity (Acts 15:1–29). At the opposite extreme, however, the age-long tradition, far wider than the Judeo-Christian teaching, that cannibalism is to be forbidden, is as binding today as it ever was.

We know, however, that on occasion even the traditional ban against cannibalism is breached, perhaps for justifiable cause. Whereas the taboo was not violated where one might expect—in the concentration camps of World War II—there is the much publicized occasion, in a recent popular novel and in the film based on it, when a plane crashed in the high Andes in South America and those who lived through the initial accident survived only by eating the flesh of a dead comrade.

We are not recalling this to debate the rightness of their act. We are interested in pointing out that even the tradition against cannibalism, so universally held, is subject to challenge by an appeal to what lies *behind* the tradition: *the experience of the community*. This is true of every tradition.

Every tradition lasts because the community which carries

it on—be it a small band, isolated in the snowfields of the high Andes, or the entire human race—finds it necessary for preserving what it perceives to be of value to its life. Traditions are related to human wholeness, and as long as the community understands this, it will at its best maintain them.

Why cease circumcision and continue the taboo against cannibalism? The answer seems so obvious, but it is just as true in a less obvious comparison: Why drop the prohibition against the ordination of women to the priesthood, but continue baptizing with the water in the name of the Trinity? It is because the community makes the choice in the light of its judgment of what best serves its goals. The canon of the New Testament itself, for example, is what it is, in the final analysis, only because the Christian community decided that those particular twenty-seven books would be included and no others.

The small band of people, lost in the high Andes, acted against the tradition of countless centuries and the vast majority of the human race and ate one of their own. It was a community decision, based upon its perception of what best served its present experience and goal of survival. We all do the same thing, when we are at our best and not neglecting the quest for human wholeness—although in a much less dramatic manner.

The question of tradition is then pushed back to the nature of the community of faith. It begins with that community's awareness of the ways in which past meaning illumines the present experience. The church in Western Europe, of which the Anglican communion is a part, has always understood this clearly. We have believed that the way in which tradition is authoritative changes as the community, living faithfully in the present, seeks to draw on the past to understand where it might be going in an unknown future. We cannot live as if time stopped moving.

The word "tradition" itself is a Latin word, which comes from the Greek *paradosis*. The *paradosis* is the *event* of bequeathing or handing down from one generation to another. The emphasis is not so much on the thing bequeathed but on the continuity of action. The act of handing down is one in which there is a basic awareness of continuity within a community *as a community*. This is why the Second Vatican Council, the most notable Christian gathering of the twentieth century, spoke of tradition not as *something* passed along, but as a *continuity of faith as lived*.

What continues is a faithfulness: a style of openness, trust, and intimacy between the community and God. What is bequeathed to each successive generation of the Church is the vulnerability of two subjects, God and God's people, who disclose themselves one to the other. It is the life of the lover and the beloved, as so beautifully described in the Song of Songs.

Marriage counselors tell us that a good marriage begets good marriages. Children who learn from the model of their parents the intimacy of a genuine marital bond are far more likely than those who come from broken or unhappy homes to have the kind of creative marriage of which the Bible speaks as the symbol of the relationship between God and humanity. The tradition of the church is faith as lived, and it is that faith which it seeks to teach its children in each successive generation. To cling to the externals of tradition, without ever understanding that they are derivative of this intimate relationship, can be the deepest betrayal of the inner meaning of tradition.

Tradition is then the *passing on of a spirit of realtionship* that we know as faith. Only secondarily and derivatively is tradition a matter of content. As content it takes its most profound and enduring form in ritual and myth. "For the tradition which I handed on to you," says Paul, "came to me from the Lord himself; that the Lord Jesus, on the night of his arrest, took bread and, after giving thanks to God, broke it and said: 'This is my body . . .'" (I Cor. 11:23–24). The most significant and long-lasting traditions we have are at the level of symbol. It is hard to imagine the Christian community ever forsaking the tradition of the action of Baptism and the Eucharist, even though the words and structure of the rite may change. The account of the life, death, and resurrection of Jesus is the *content* of tradition at its deepest level.

It is certainly not consistent with the church's experience to suggest that as we move away from that tradition which merges into the very faith of the community's interpersonal experience of God we find the same unchanging authority. The formulae, the systems, the laws, all inevitably change as some are dropped and new ones added. It is perhaps the printing press and other means of preserving the past in an objective manner that have made us more aware and sometimes alarmed at the evolution of tradition. No early Christian would know, much less expect, the words of the liturgy to remain the same from Sunday to Sunday, much less from generation to generation, as we do.

At this level and in this sense revelation is continuous. New traditions come into being and old traditions fade. God will not be bound by our past understanding, and God expects of the apostolic church as much responsibility for its experience of God in the present as God did in the first, fourth, twelfth, or sixteenth centuries. Certainly this is unnerving for all of us, since there are few persons who do not take comfort in having a secure vision of who they are and what might happen. It is not, however, to that kind of rest that God calls us when he leads us into being.

· 7 ·

A Style of Belief

There is a story told of Augustine of Hippo walking on the shores of the Mediterranean Sea. He came across a little child, who had dug a hole in the sand. He watched the young boy and noticed how he was running back and forth between the small hole and the sea carrying water, which he poured into the hole. The child appeared to be exhausted, but persisted at his work. Augustine, out of kindness for the weary boy, said to him, "Child, what are you doing?" Recognizing him, the child replied, "Holy bishop, I am pouring that sea into this hole." "Why, that's absurd," replied Augustine, "don't you see how small the hole is you have dug and how vast the sea is?" But the child was really an angel given the appearance of a child and sent to enlighten Augustine. He replied, "Yes, holy bishop, and so is your mind so very small and the knowledge of God so vast."

The language of belief is limited and can never encompass the whole being of God. We have no direct or complete access to the knowledge of the transcendent. Our knowledge of God is always a knowledge as *related to the human subject*. We can only speak of God by speaking of ourselves in the context of our culture. A culture is a people's learned, shared understanding and ways. We are shaped by our culture and in turn we give shape to our culture. Every attempt to represent our experience of God reflects the character of the culture in which we live. Statements of belief are expressions of faith, but they are limited by our time and place in a particular culture. Belief is always relative to history, and to our experience.

Experience is everything that has happened and is happening to us. But if we are aware of our experience at all, it is only a very small portion of it. Humans are physically limited in regard to how much of their experience can be sensed, and they are conditioned by their culture to be aware of even less. A dog whistle is an example of our physical limitations. It is constructed on the principle that there are certain high frequencies of sound waves, imperceptible to the human ear, which a dog can hear. An example of cultural limitations would be someone whose language does not have the equivalent of the word "orange" in it—as in the color orange. Experiments have shown that when presented with a color that we who speak an Indo-European tongue would call "orange," people for whom no such word exists in their language would call it "red" or "yellow," depending on which of those two colors predominates in the tint or blend they are seeing.

We all screen or "edit" our particular knowledge. People brought up in different cultures learn as children, without ever knowing that they have done so, to screen out one set of experiences and to pay close attention to another. Consider, for example, that in the Arctic there is no horizon separating earth and sky. Visibility in the snow is all but nonexistent, yet the Eskimo can travel across miles of such terrain because of an awareness of the relationship between the contours of the land, types of snow, wind, salt air, and cracks in the ice. However, the same Eskimo most likely would find it difficult to travel confidently through the streets of New York City.

The experience is "there," whether or not we are conscious of it. In fact, we are never aware of much of it, much less all of it. Like the Soviet astronaut who announced that he had been out in space and had seen no God, if people say that God is not part of their experience, they are only saying that *they are not conscious* of God in their experience. If people say there is nothing in their experience that indicates that humans have evolved over the last million years or so, it could be that such people have not been willing or able to make themselves available to the experience from which such a belief could emerge.

Meaning is an internally consistent, significant representation of experience. Meaning is the sense we make of experience. If God is present in our experience, as in the faith we hold, then meaning is our representation of that experience. It is our identification of experience through images stored in our memory, but it is also much more. It is the result of our drawing upon our present environment to make sense of what is happening to us.

Building meaning is like building a house. One of the significant steps in the evolution of humanity begins at that point in which people became aware of their need for shelter and translated that need into the action of building a shelter. Archaeologists claim to have found on the beaches of the French Riviera the signs of shelter-building by our ancestors 400,000 years ago. Since then we have used the memory of the houses in which we grew up to construct houses for ourselves.

You can see Mayan Indians in the Yucatan today living in stick-and-mud shelters just like those depicted in carvings in the ancient pyramids of their ancestors. The Bedouin nomads on the Arabian deserts live in the same kind of goat-hair tents their ancestors lived in when Jesus walked on earth. A thousand years ago in western Europe people lived in wattle huts in time of peace and in the stone towers of their local lords in time of war. When their descendants came to North America they soon left those houses behind and came to adopt, in many areas, the log cabins built by some native Americans, since trees were in abundance and stone hard to work. Today some of us live in wooden homes, some in brick houses, and a few in stone houses, depending on what is most readily available and what we remember a house "ought to look like." The need for shelter is absolute. There are, however, no universal house specifications and blueprints. A house is a meaning determined to a major extent by the culture in which we live.

Meaning is peculiar to individuals as members of social groups. Meaning arises as we interact with others at a given point in the history of our society. This is why meaning, like belief, is relative and pluralistic. One cannot have a meaning which extends much beyond what is possible within a given culture at a given time.

We say "much beyond." Clearly someone straining for new understandings will tax the language available to construct new models of understanding. But this straining at the limitations of the language can only go so far. St. Paul, for example, may be rightly faulted for his attitudes toward women and slaves, but it would be unrealistic to expect him, as a citizen of the first century A.D., to think otherwise. Our experience of God can change a culture; we are not the captive of the culture. But we need to avoid illusions as to how dramatic that influence might be.

Because meaning is relative to the society in which it is constructed, it also assumes various forms in different cultures. God is present to all humanity. But Buddhists do not usually have visions of the Blessed Virgin and Christians are unlikely to have them of the Buddha.

The relationship between meaning and experience cannot be understood until we take into account the social conditioning of all beliefs. All beliefs are relative to the point in history in which they are made, as well as the particular culture out of which they emerge. This is not to lapse into a gross relativism. Meaning has many levels. Although the only meaning which is absolute is that in the mind of God, some meaning is closer to God's mind than others. If it were not so there would be no need for theology and we would all be isolated from one another by a fearsome subjectivism. The struggle to discern God's meaning in the midst of historical meaning is what thinking humans are all about. The Bible is a clear illustration.

The blood-thirsty nomadic God of Joshua, who led the tribes of Israel into Palestine in the latter half of the thirteenth millennium B.C., makes a stark contrast to the universal God of Jesus Ben Sirach, the second century B.C. Hellenistic cosmopolite, who wrote Ecclesiasticus. For Joshua's God, the greatest virtue was to kill the enemies of God; for Jesus Ben Sirach's God, it was to be wise. The incredible difference is a matter of belief influenced by history and culture. But we choose the God of Jesus Ben Sirach because he is more like the God of Jesus of Nazareth.

Jesus is the norm, because we believe that through him God chose to reconcile the whole world to himself (Col. 1:20). This is a fundamental statement and about as close to the mind of God as one can get—although each word is open to argument. The next two sections will explore the truth of this statement in the light of contemporary experience. It has much to say—perhaps everything to say—about a Christian style of belief.

But it is also clear that in the New Testament there are differing beliefs about Jesus. For the Palestinian Jewish Christians, Jesus is the risen Messiah, who shall one day return to judge us all. For the Hellenistic Jewish Christians, Jesus is the risen Messiah, who is now Lord and rules from heaven until the day when he shall return. For the Gentile Christians, Jesus is the incarnate preexistent Son of God, who is now Lord and rules from heaven until the day when he shall return. Those are very different beliefs, but the same faith.

Plurality of belief is present not only among differing religious communities, but within the Christian community. Throughout its history Christian belief can be explained in terms of the point in history and the place in culture of those who express the community's beliefs. For example, the systematic theology of Thomas Aquinas, who wrote in the thirteenth century, did a magnificent job of giving meaning to the Christian experience of his time. And while the First Vatican Council (1870) made his conceptualization of Christian belief final, it could not last. It could not stand in the face of a people, living in a different point in history and in another culture. And so the Second Vatican Council ninety-odd years later backed off from making Aquinas the final authority. All belief statements are similar to those made by St. Thomas Aquinas. They are human historical efforts to give meaning to our experience. As such they are relative to time and place, and pluralistic.

If we wish to understand what people in another culture

and time understood from their experience, we have to enter as best we can into *their* memory, language, social world, pain, and hopes. Since we cannot actually live in a time and culture other than our own, we can at best have an empathic relationship with the understandings of others. This should give us pause before we think of some other place and period as a "golden age." It is a logistical impossibility to be a nineteenth-century Anglo-Catholic, a sixteenth-century Lutheran, or a thirteenth-century Franciscan in the late twentieth century. Nor should one want to be.

Each age must work at reconstituting the meaning of the experience of God. To abrogate this responsibility is a serious offense. This is not to argue for superficial "relevance." Opponents of theological change have sometimes quipped, "He who marries the spirit of the age is doomed soon to be a widower." The imagery may be amusing, but it is inappropriate. An imagery much more to the point is to say that all of us are the *children* of our age and culture. Our parents shall die and we must live our own lives. As Carl Jung once said, we are not mature until our father dies. Whether or not he meant that literally, the point is that we cannot claim our life as our own until we cease living it in terms of our father's meaning. To fail to engage in the never-ending process of reconstituting the meaning of the experience of God is, in this light, a refusal to grow up.

The Truth of God

The late bishop of California James A. Pike (1913–1969), when he was chaplain at Columbia University, told of a woman student who came to him and said: "I no longer can believe in God." Pike asked her, "Tell about the God in whom you no longer believe." When she had finished, he remarked, "I don't believe in that God either."

Sometimes we have to reconceive God before we can believe in him. Belief is relative to our culture and times. Statements about God are the "clothing" which we put on the God whom, in faith, we know. But the clothing comes from our culturally conditioned memory, and from our culture itself.

The world in which Jesus Christ lived, was raised, and died did *not* possess one, homogeneous culture. Jesus was reared in a relatively isolated Jewish town. There he probably knew an almost pure Palestinian Jewish culture. But a more cosmopolitan city, such as Jerusalem, would be much more influenced by the prevailing stronger culture, known as Hellenism. "Hellenism" is the name we give to an eclectic cultural movement, which began with the conquest of the eastern end of the Mediterranean basin by Alexander the Great. Alexander was not a very profound thinker, although he was a remarkably successful general. He was infatuated with things Greek and the cultural movement which he begot was ostensibly and predominantly Greek in spirit, though it was capable of incorporating all kinds of ideas into an eclectic unity of manners and outlook. The resultant "Hellenism" had a profound impact on the Roman Empire, *including particularly the early Christian church.*

In Hellenistic culture the physical world was a shadow of the real world. Furthermore, the universe was conceived spatially, not temporally (as in Hebrew thought). Their God was a spatial divinity—"up there." God was the cause of all things and, therefore, knew all things, but God was so distant that he was inaccessible to humans. Hellenism was an excessively masculine culture, so it is no surprise that the philosopher's God was of pure, rational mind. There was no emotion to him. He did not suffer. He legitimated the absolute power of the Roman emperor and, therefore, was all-powerful just like the emperor. Time was considered part of the human problem; therefore, God was timeless or eternal. Change was an illusion to Hellenistic philosophy, because creation was cyclical. It did not go anywhere; it repeated what had been. Therefore, God did not change. He was above it all.

In Hellenistic thought, human beings were made up of three parts: body, soul, and mind. Each one in turn was better than the other, and the parts were divisible. To be most human was to be spirit or mind, because this was the part closest to God. The created order emanated from God in a hierarchical form and, therefore, while God was everywhere, he seemed to be in some places more than others.

Perhaps this description of the God of Hellenistic culture sounds familiar. Up until a generation ago it was the God represented in most theology books. Hellenism was a very strong influence in the ancient world and it quickly overwhelmed the God of Jewish culture.

The New Testament, which we might expect to have been influenced dominantly by Jewish culture, often represents the God of Hellenism. The author of James, for example, writes, "With him [God] there is no variation, or shadow due to change. Of his set purpose, own will he brought us forth by the word of truth that we should be a kind of first fruits of his creatures" (Jas. 1:17−18). St. Paul writes of an experience of his own in terms of a clear Hellenistic cosmology. "I knew a man in Christ fourteen years ago . . . snatched up into the third heaven" (II Cor. 12:2; translation, the authors). The Apostle Paul also uses Hellenistic categories to argue the difference between the first Adam and the second Adam, who is Christ (I Cor. 15:44−50). Unless we understand the philosophical distinction in Hellenism between a soul-person and a spirit-person, his argument is at best obscure.

Hebrews, which culturally belies its name, bases its entire argument on the Hellenistic notion of the universe. God is he "for whom and through whom all things exist." (Heb. 2:10). His work has been finished "ever since the world was created" (Heb. 4:3). The present created world is a shadow or representation of the real, which is in heaven (Heb. 9:24, 10:1). The unknown author of Hebrews has a great deal in common with a Jewish philosopher of the first century A.D., who attempted to translate Jewish belief in the categories of Hellenistic philosophy. This same Jewish philosopher also resembles the author of the Fourth Gospel, who in using the image of the Word (Logos) was borrowing directly from the prevailing Gentile culture. All three foreshadow the Christian apologists of the second century, who accommodated Christian thought to a dominant cultural image of Hellenism.

There is nothing wrong in this accommodation. In fact, it was necessary and good. But moderns must not confuse the heart of faith with this clothing of accommodation. Although Pike does not tell us, we can guess that the unhappiness of the Columbia student with God might well have been the results of her effort to accommodate the Christian-Hellenistic God with her experience. Much of the discomfort we moderns feel about particular Christian beliefs results from this confusion.

Recall that earlier we raised the problem of someone explaining the death of a young woman in a meaningless traffic accident by saying it is part of the mysterious will of God. In a culture where arbitrary decisions were imposed upon hapless people, perhaps such an explanation would coincide with the cultural expectations. But they violate deeply our sense of justice and love today.

Similarly, to believe that life is only a cosmic drama in which God has written the script in every detail before it all began is difficult. Does God let the world evolve, knowing that it is going to end up just as he plans? Such a contention creates an unnecessary dualism—God up there and we down here—and makes it difficult for us to understand how God can love us if God is not present with us. We doubt that the Puritan God, who is a particularly stern form of the Hellenistic God, fits in a helpful way our contemporary image of a universe evolving.

It also leaves many of us asking why we bother to offer prayers of intercession or petition, if God already has everything worked out. The implication is that God either does not know what is best and needs to have his mind changed, or perhaps he is an indulgent grandfather. The further suggestion that this is God's way of testing us, which is presumably consistent with the Hellenistic God, is of little comfort.

Beliefs about God derived from Hellenism are the creation of that culture's deep commitment to a particular worldview. The Hellenistic God died when the dramatic shift from a cosmocentric (beginning from above) to an anthropocentric (beginning from below) worldview began to take place about two hundred years ago. It passed away with the demise of the established churches, the absolute sovereignty of individual rulers, and the concept of the "white man's burden." Our problem today lies in the fact that we are not aware that many inherited beliefs about God are the product of a cultural worldview which neither Jesus Christ knew nor we late twentieth-century people possess. We can lament its death, but that has nothing to do with the growing evidence that the Hellenistic God ill-fits our contemporary worldview.

What does the present culture predicate of God? There is no simple answer to that question, because there is no one, homogeneous culture. We can at best expect a variety of beliefs, some of them in conflict with one another. However, in our culture God is perhaps best understood as person. God is with us in our joys and in our suffering. God is an utterly unselfish parent or friend. God is loving and just. God empathizes with us. God comforts us in our fear. God sustains us for a better world. It is not surprising that theologians today question more and more the idea that God is timeless, never changing, and incapable of emotion. Human beings are no longer seen as separate from or against God; but rather all of creation is considered a part of God, and we humans are active participants in the completion of creation. One might suspect that God will be seen less and less as a masculine, "sky law-giver" and will become more the androgynous (a conjoining of the masculine with the feminine) "earth parent."

If we predicate to God the qualities of a desirable subject, we also need to understand that God is infinitely more. God is that which we cannot conceive. God lies beyond the abyss into which we gaze at the horizon of our knowing.

It is in the infinite *more* that contemporary humans place God's vision for creation. God is *purposively creating*. The evolution of the universe is not a matter of chance; it is not meaningless. God may be affected by his own action in creation—God may suffer; God may change; God may experience time—since time is created, had a beginning, and will have an end. Perhaps God can experience time as God experiences each one of us—but creation itself is a willful action on God's part.

Most important, the central symbol of our Christian belief, Jesus Christ, is more congruent with the predications of God that are emerging in our culture than those we inherited from the Hellenistic culture.

The Meaningfulness of Christ

Jesus Christ is the central, primordial symbol of the experience of God for those who consider themselves to be Christians. Christians affirm that the norm by which every experience of God is to be interpreted is the symbol of Jesus Christ. This is precisely what the Fourth Evangelist means when he puts into the mouth of Jesus in reply to Philip's request that he might be shown the Father, "He who has seen me has seen the Father" (Jn. 14:9).

It is important that we seek to keep the symbol of Jesus Christ as clean of cultural accretions as possible. Only then can we see what relevance Jesus Christ can have to contemporary humanity. Jesus of Nazareth is known to us today as one who preached and lived the coming of the Kingdom and as the one raised from the grave. He has anticipated for us all our quest for fulfillment. Jesus Christ is the creative transformation of our lives.

Christ is the symbol of God. But in the early centuries of the church the prevailing Hellenistic culture shaped the God revealed in Christ. Whereas it does no good to fault our spiritual ancestors, we do have the obligation to reflect anew as to what we can truly believe about God.

We humans perceive ourselves—if we reflect on ourselves at all—as unfinished. We all sense in the meaning of our experience an absence of fulfillment. As Christians we speak of Jesus Christ as a symbol of fulfillment, and thus we call him our Savior or Redeemer. Before the Christian community asks who Jesus Christ is it experiences him as one who speaks to our longing for completion. When Jesus asked his disciples at Caesarea Philippi, "Who do men say that the Son of man is?" (Mt. 16:13), the disciples had been walking with him for a long time. It is hard to say what caused great multitudes, as well as Peter and Andrew, John, and James, and others we know by name, to leave their work, their families, and their homes to wander about the countryside with Jesus. It seems probable that it was a recognition that this man offered them the promise of fulfillment which they sought.

Does Jesus Christ make a difference today? That question is somewhat more complicated than it has been made to appear. We have already said he is a symbol of fulfillment to the Christian community, but who is "he"?

In the mid-nineteenth century theologians made a distinction between the Jesus of history and the Christ of faith. It is very hard to know the son of the carpenter, Jesus of Nazareth, as his companions knew him. The New Testament is the product of oral and written tradition evolving over several generations. The historical Jesus lies largely hidden within successive layers of words and interpretations.

Over the last century some believers have despaired of discovering the Jesus of history, but they have found that of little ultimate importance. The Jesus we know, they point out, is really the Christ of faith, the symbol that speaks to our personal longing. He is a particular personalization of humanity's universal longing.

Jesus was a man possessed by a hope for the Kingdom of God. And the Kingdom is an image of human fulfillment. In Jesus the Kingdom is not only preached—it is lived. His words were identical with his being. Quite simply he considered himself an instrument in the establishment of God's Kingdom.

The Christ of faith is the symbol of what comes to fulfill the self and the world we experience as unfinished. He is the expectation of an order in the future, which will free us from the absurdity of the present. To know the Jesus of history is to be confronted by the Kingdom of God (the completion of all things) and to discover the power to join in the process of transforming the present into that fulfilled future. Jesus is aware of himself in some sense as the embodiment of the order that is to come.

As we contemplate the anticipated fulfillment of our lives and history, death remains the overwhelming problem. We cannot believe that the power of love which we experience even in this unfulfilled life is, in the end, to be overcome by the nothingness of death. We cannot separate death and evil. We know evil; we succumb to evil; and we do evil. We also die—fully and totally. We fear we have no "immortal soul."

The Jesus Christ of the New Testament is one who, like us, dies. The cross is no accident on the way to the empty tomb; it is the prerequisite of the resurrection. He is one with us, and by virtue of this fact offers us hope.

In the resurrection of Jesus we believe that we have an authentic witness to the promise of a new future free from evil and death. The resurrection is not "just a symbol" for us—some kind of fiction that gullible minds of superstitious primitives believed in the face of overwhelming fear. It is the inevitable consequence of who Jesus is.

God in Jesus Christ enters the chaos of our despair and death—and prevails. He is the divine representation of our faith in creativity and order. And he does this as a particular flesh-and-blood person in history: Jesus of Nazareth.

The resurrection is, therefore, the anticipation of what shall someday be for us all: the fulfillment of our humanity. The Kingdom which Jesus Christ preached and embodied is here now in his risen presence; it shall be in all creation.

This means for us that death is not the end. We do not face annihilation, any more than did Christ upon the Cross. In Jesus Christ we have the promise of our future, not as some philosophical abstraction, but as personal existence into everlasting life. This is what we affirm in the creeds, when we state our belief in the resurrection of the body—that as Christ dies and was raised so shall we be. What that future will be like, however, we do not now know.

Christians and the Faith of Others

All religious faith is founded in a person, a moral imperative, a transcendent reality, and other nonpropositions. Our Christian propositions are like all religious belief—an expression of that faith in the context of our time and culture.

It does not seem reasonable to maintain that the Gospel can be purged of all cultural overlays. (There are, of course, some people who believe sincerely that if one reads the Bible one will find an evident, coherent, unified set of beliefs given by God which transcends all cultural and historical relationships.) Nor does it seem believable that all which is not explicitly related to Jesus Christ is to be rejected as irredeemably flawed. (There are also sincere people who believe in this way.)

At the same time an absolute relativism seems equally unacceptable. Such popular sayings as "every church has many windows" (implying that every religion has its own "windows"), or "there is a little bit of good and a little bit of bad in everyone" (implying that no one is better than anyone else—a frightening suggestion!), or "there is more than one road to heaven" (implying that we will all get there no matter what we believe) are pure sentimentality. Less sentimental, but essentially equivalent, is the position that there is no criterion outside the self for judging value and, therefore, no basis upon which to say whether or not one set of beliefs is better than another.

But there is indeed a criterion for judging value, and everyone operates on the basis of some such criterion, whether or not they are willing to acknowledge it. This criterion is the absolute and universal faith that there is an order to experience; a certain moral direction to life; that someday the purpose of life shall be fulfilled; and that we ought to work for that day.

It is also apparent that some beliefs are better able to give expression to this faith and, thereby, to engender deeper faith in the possibility of a creative transformation of this present life. These become the ground for action that promotes a better existence where love is shared and justice prevails in accord with our primal ethical intuition. Such belief *frees* us from the prison of our present alienation and oppression. Certainly this is a Christian expectation of belief. But belief can have the very opposite effect. Our beliefs can result from the fear of the responsibility that freedom places on us.

Perhaps the greatest passage written by one of the greatest novelists of all time is Dostoevsky's account of the Grand Inquisitor in *The Brothers Karamazov*. At one point in Dostoevsky's tale Ivan Karamazov tells of Jesus' return to Spain at the height of the Inquisition. Every day heretics are burned to the "greater glory of God," and when Jesus comes among the people, healing them, offering them hope, the Grand Inquisitor arrests him and declares his intention to burn him also. And as Ivan explains, it is out of love for the people that the Grand Inquisitor does this. For the burden of freedom, as the Inquisitor says to Jesus, is too much for humans to bear. "They will cry aloud at least that the truth is not in Thee," observes the Inquisitor, "for they could not have been left in greater confusion and suffering than Thou hast caused, laying upon them so many cares and unanswerable problems." They would prefer by far to believe in the certain bread the Inquisitor gives than the painful freedom Jesus Christ offers.

In having the nonbeliever, Ivan, attack his believing brother, Alyosha Karamazov, with this cynical story, Dostoevsky is telling us a truth we all know. We are at our best when we have the faith to be free and to risk the new. This is the ground for all hope for it offers the possibility of love, without which we all die. Alyosha, who stands for faith, is the hero in this novel, not because he "wins," but because he embodies what is most true about people. Alyosha's belief is *better* than Ivan's nonbelief.

The beliefs that deepen our faith and thereby give us the power to be free to risk the uncertain future are better beliefs than any others. Granted, this criterion provides us with no easy quantifiable formula by which we can readily measure another's belief. It demands judgment grounded in faith. There is no way for us to "get off the hook." We have to risk saying that this belief is better than another without having any final assurance that it is so.

But notice that this is no arbitrary, exclusive process, in

which we exclude from God's presence all save that very small minority that might agree with us. It recognizes the plurality of belief and belief's relativity to culture, while still insisting that there is a basis for evaluation. There are those who have no knowledge of Jesus Christ and yet are people of faith, hope, and love. In other words, there are people who hold no distinctively Christian beliefs, yet God, who is in Christ, is a saving presence to them.

What the Christian brings to the possibility of universal faith is a symbol of Jesus Christ which transcends culture. The Christ of faith is not ours to possess. He is free of our culture, and thereby free to take on a form peculiar to the culture and consequent beliefs of many others. Indeed, we find our own commitment to God in terms of our own beliefs deepened by experiencing the distinctively different beliefs of someone else who has an equally authentic faith.

We need not enter into a dialogue with a Buddhist or a member of Islam to win or to lose. Our intention ought to be that we both shall win. It is highly doubtful, given the cultural contexts in which Buddhism exists, that such dialogue will result in the baptism of many who were previously Buddhists. It is improbable that it will result in theological agreement between the representatives of two very disparate systems of belief. It is altogether possible, however, that in our points of contact we will find enrichment which will flow over into the beliefs of each religion.

Those points of contact between the major world religions have been variously identified. Friedrich Heiler, a noted German historian of religion, distinguishes in Judaism, Islam, Zoroastrian Mazdianism, Hinduism, Buddhism, Taoism, and Christianity several areas of common belief, which form a basis for serious dialogue.

First, there is a belief in the reality of the transcendent, whatever it may be called: "eternal truth," "true being," the "other," or the "holy."

Second, the transcendent is believed also to be immanent in human hearts.

Third, this transcendent and immanent reality is the highest good, which becomes the goal for the striving of all human religions.

4) Fourth, the reality of the divine is ultimate love.

5) Fifth, the way of man to God is one of sacrifice. The surrender of the self in some way is involved in the living of every religion we have named.

6) Sixth, all religions teach that in loving one's neighbor, even one's enemies, without limitation, one is loving God.

7) Seventh, the supreme way to God is love. It is the love of God that leads to union with God, whatever that union is believed to be.

The acknowledgment and exploration of the common beliefs form a basis for further confrontation with those beliefs with which we radically differ. If belief is expressive of our experience of God within the limits of our memory and culture, then this confrontation can open our eyes to aspects in our experience of which we may not be aware.

In a world where all the human family shares common needs and longings, it only makes sense that all who have faith in a transcendent reality which calls them to just love, share their beliefs, grow together into a deeper humanity, and work together to fulfill their visions of life's potential.

There is a value for us all in the dialogue between Christianity and other religions. The witness of the church is not to the exclusive presence of God to baptized Christians alone, but to God's mediation of himself through the resurrection of Jesus, fulfilling the aspirations of all believing people. God is present to all. All are saved who give themselves in faith, hope, and love to God whether or not they have an explicit commitment to Christ. Yet we all stand to gain if we, as witnesses to Christ, share our belief with others and they with us.

There is a great deal of ignorance in the world—indeed in our nation—about what is a Christian believer. The believers are as much at fault as anyone, for they have often made their style of belief an unnecessary stumbling block. We have not seen it as a style—one option among many—for giving substance to our conviction that God is in Christ Jesus. The dialogue between private belief and the world needs to face with painful clarity the process by which we move from faith to belief, noting both the necessity that we do so and the presumption with which we do it.

The best test, of course, of our faith and its resultant beliefs is their fruits: the action that springs from them. The First Evangelist reminds us that we will be recognized by our fruits (Mt. 7:20), and not by the cleverness of our beliefs, as necessary as they are. What we make of our world is not the ultimate issue; it is what we do about it in the light of what we make of it that communicates.

· 8 ·

The Consequences of Belief

A seminarian studying for the priesthood recounted a field
education experience in a children's detention center. One
day a staff person passed him on the grounds and said, "Hi
there. I want to ask you something. As a psychologist, I
know what I am doing here. I also know what the social
worker does, the guards, the secretaries, the cooks, and the
doctors. But what do *you* do here?" That's a question which
surfaces quite frequently these days. Sometimes it is sincerely curious and at other times hostile.

At public gatherings priests frequently have one of two
experiences. On the one hand, there are those people who
treat priests with a kind of condescending deference. The
content and the tone of conversations within their hearing
take on a polite, nonoffensive quality. The priest is treated as
one might treat an elderly maiden aunt who has come for a
visit. On the other hand, there is a growing tendency to
challenge the priest and the priest's knowledge by talking
about "religion" without recognizing the priest as having
any knowledge on the subject.

Not long ago at a cocktail party two members of a university faculty were comparing two church-sponsored second-
ary schools. The observation was made, in the hearing of a
priest who was also a guest, that one school was to be preferred to the other because it has not let its church affiliation
interfere with its life; it offered a "completely secular education." The point was not offered as an opinion or as an item
for discussion. It was intended as an obvious conclusion.

The priest was not even asked for an opinion, although everyone present knew that he had chosen, at some financial sacrifice, to keep his son in the "more religious" prep school.

There has been a growing movement in some quarters of the culture (and even the church) to believe that "secular is better." The continuing popularity of Harvey Cox's *The Secular City* is a symptom of this opinion. Written almost two decades ago, the Harvard theologian maintained that a secular world frees Christ to work within society. The institutional church, according to this view, finds it impossible to live for others. This is why—as the simplistic analysis goes—Jesus broke with the religious establishment and why we should welcome not only the disestablishment of the church, but also the demythologization of the church's teaching.

There is every good reason to understand such a reaction among intelligent, concerned persons. It is not difficult to prove that the church has in fact opposed freedom. The church has often limited people's freedom so as to protect them from a pain the church assumes they cannot bear. The church has often used religion as an "opiate." We must never forget that one motive for making Christians out of the black slaves in the South was to render them more "docile."

The world has a long memory. It recalls well the condemnation of Galileo in the seventeenth century for demonstrating that the earth revolves around the sun, rather than the other way around. It knows that John Calvin in the sixteenth century burned Michael Servetus at the stake for teaching the circulation of the blood. It recalls that only Charles Darwin's personal wealth prevented nineteenth-century Anglican scholars from doing anything more than vilifying him in print for his theory of evolution and natural selection. *The Index of Forbidden Books*, which the Roman Catholic church formally published for the first time in 1559 and continued to publish until 1966, still rankles those people who are concerned for the free pursuit of truth. It was only recently that Pierre Teilhard de Chardin was forbidden by the Jesuit order to publish his most significant works. As late as 1962 we were warned about his teachings.

The Christian church is frequently and legitimately charged with siding with political oppression; the Roman Catholic church was the ally of the French monarchy at the end of the eighteenth century; the Episcopal church in the colonies supported George III. In 1917 the Russian Orthodox church met in solemn conclave to discuss the appropriate occasions for wearing yellow vestments while revolution swept the streets. Today the Dutch Reformed church in South Africa provides theological assurance for the horror of apartheid in South Africa. It does not matter whether these issues are representative of Christian thought or not, they are the issues recalled by the secular mind. And its representatives have made a "declaration of independence" for the freedom of the spirit. Religion must go in the name of liberation and humanity.

But what does it mean to live a secular life? What is it that a "secular school" *necessarily* has that is to be preferred over what a "religious school" *necessarily* has? How is it that the secular world offers a freedom that the Christian world denies by the virtue of what each one is? It would actually seem that the secularist is no freer than the religionist. As a matter of fact, the life of the secularist often seems to be a good bit less meaningful. One senses a poverty of spirit in secular humanity that makes people vulnerable to the occult, to astrology, and to a host of other sect and cult groups. Can a strictly secular state, such as the Soviet Union, offer to the Russian people anything as meaningful as Christmas or Easter? What is it about *Walden II* or *Ecotopia* that leaves us yawning?

It is not too surprising that Harvey Cox found that less than three years after he wrote *The Secular City* he had to write *The Feast of Fools* (1969) and most recently *The Seduction of the Spirit.* While neither was a recantation of his first thesis, they confront and move beyond his original romantic notion of the glorious secular world.

Some have chosen to explain the current, new enthusiasm for the sacred as a retreat from the disappointments of social activism. It could be better explained as an awareness that something was missing in our enthusiasm for the secular.

What is that "something"? It is, as this chapter's title expresses it, "the consequences of belief"! The secular mind tends to think of freedom as freedom *from*. Nonbelievers and disbelievers are apt to say they have no need to believe. They are free from these kinds of obligations. They have no "holes" for God to "fill up." They are self-sufficient; therefore their moments of dependence must be carefully guarded so as not to attribute purpose and meaning to anything other than themselves. They are free *from* others, free *from* their cultural past. As a result they are incapable of answers to their most fundamental questions about existence.

Believers are more inclined to think of freedom as freedom *to* acknowledge that they are not self-sufficient, that they have the freedom to live for someone and something other than themselves.

What is missing from the secular age gets excluded when we have to defend our freedom. Many a tyranny, many a book burning, many an iconoclast were defended in the name of freedom. We need to enable freedom, not try to defend or guard it. Freedom is life in the unknown. Freedom can only be pursued if we have an appreciation of mystery. *Close out the mystery in life and you destroy freedom.*

Rediscovering the Sacred

The sacred can be utterly dehumanizing. The words of Amos have as authentic a ring today as they did 1,700 years ago.

> "I hate, I despise your feasts,
> and I take no delight in your
> solemn assemblies.
> Even though you offer me your
> burnt offerings and cereal
> offerings,
> I will not accept them,
> and the peace offerings of your
> fatted beasts
> I will not look upon.

Take away from me the noise of
    your songs;
to the melody of your harps I
    will not listen.
But let justice roll down like waters,
    and righteousness like an ever-
    flowing stream.

"Did you bring to me sacrifices and offerings the forty years in
the wilderness, O house of Israel?"

(Amos 5:21–25)

Amos rightly discerned that an imposition of the sacred can become an obstacle, rather than an aid, to God's purposes for creation. The Old Testament's abhorrence of idols is a recognition that to attribute holiness to anything other than the Word of God is to dilute seriously the power of that Word on our lives. A God who is known in sacred places, in sacred objects, and in sacred acts, a God who legitimizes society's institutions, is typically a God who sanctions the status quo, with all of its injustice and tyranny.

Devout participation in the liturgy is no excuse for a lack of charity or an insensitivity to injustice. We cannot justify who we are by our piety. We must take responsibility for our lives and for the society in which we live.

There is a healthiness in the secular critique of the misuse of the sacred. But if we are not extremely careful we will discard the baby with the bath water. The price of an extreme secularization of life is a denial of God's self-disclosure of revelation. The ancient Israelites wanted nothing to obscure the Word of God. But the contemporary secular culture has rendered God *utterly* hidden. They leave no point at which the Word of God might be unveiled. They shut their eyes and ears to the mystery that surrounds us, the mystery in which God speaks.

If God is utterly hidden from our experience, then God is not part of this world. Perhaps it was not accidental that the native Americans who saw the sacred in all kinds of places, things, and events have become symbols of the ecology movement, and their treatment at the hands of secular government has become symbolic of governmental abuse in general.

We have set in inalterable opposition priests, those who are concerned for sacred places, objects, and acts, and the prophets, those who were devoted to the pure Word of God—and justice. To do this is to misread the Scriptures. An appropriate sense of the sacred was essential for the Old Testament prophet; it was certainly a part of Jesus' ministry, and it is vital to a lively contemporary faith.

A purely secular culture cannot provide the context for God's self-disclosure and for the development of religious belief. The issue is how to achieve a renewed perception of the sacred in our world and at the same time not to diminish our freedom or obscure God's purpose for us.

The creation of oppositions needs to be avoided. The estrangement of the sacred and the profane must be eliminated. It is just not reasonable to believe that people are sacred and institutions profane; that the sacred is found in nature, but not in society; that priests are holy, while lay people are not; that the mind is spiritual, the body carnal; that there are two (to seven) sacraments, and the Holy Spirit works nowhere else; that only the beliefs of the baptized are true and those of all others are false; that the celibate life is better than the married life because it is more holy; that the world is divided between the mystics who know God and the rest of us who do not; or that one must not dance in church or think erotic thoughts.

Historically speaking, the creation of a priestly caste has worked toward an unhealthy situation. It has divided the religious communities between those who "have it" and "do it" for others, and those who do not have it and cannot do it. There is also the danger of a prophetic caste, of which precisely the same judgment can be made. There are those who have "wisdom" and who can speak for God and the rest of us have no right to reply. The tyranny of the prophets is just as real as the tyranny of the priests.

A rediscovery of the sacred demands the identification of

God with God's world. God is not ever against the world. The sacred is not ever against the profane.

To affirm the unity of the sacred and the profane is to perceive that the created order is rooted in the mystery of God. Anything and everything which serves the fulfillment of God's vision for creation is rooted in the transcendent. It is this awareness that lies behind the admonition of the author of I Peter when he writes: "Submit yourselves to every human institution for the sake of the Lord, whether to the sovereign as supreme, or to the governor as his deputy" (I Pet. 2:13). The fact that three verses later he adds a call to live as free persons (I Pet. 2:16) is the proper complement to the first injunction.

Our earliest ancestors identified themselves with the world of their senses and, at the same time, assumed a reality to what they sensed. Behind every object—be it tree, brook, rock, king, father, mother—there was another subject: its "spirit." We are inclined to consider this way of thinking of things as naive. But for our ancient ancestors the world was transparent; divinity shone through. For us the world has become unintelligible.

On our journey to secular sophistication we divided public life between the kingdom of the spirit and the kingdom of the world. We gave the former to the church and the latter to secular rulers. We divided human nature into the "spiritual" and the "material." While we cannot regain the perceptions of our ancestors we can try to strip away some of our preconceptions and preconditions. We can perceive the inner subject that lies behind the objective world of our experience. We are calling for a rediscovery of the sacred. We need to refuse to either cling to the separation of the sacred and the profane or to lapse into the meaninglessness of a one-dimensional, secular understanding of reality. Instead we need to grope for the inner dimension of all experience through a revitalization of our imaginations or intuitive modes of consciousness.

The imagination is not just one inherent capacity, apart from others which we cultivate within individuals. It is the attitude of the whole person. Imagination is an openness to the possibilities of all experience, so that the mind may be illumined in ways independent of stereotypical thinking or ideological presuppositions. It is looking at the world as did the little child of whom Jesus spoke (Mt. 18:1—4). Stereotypical thinking and ideological presuppositions were characteristic of those whom Jesus described as having a hardened heart or closed mind (Mt. 19:8, Mk. 3:5, 10:5, 16:15).

Furthermore, a rediscovery of the sacred does not allow us to divide the world into the "ordinary" and the "extraordinary" or to speak of *two* kinds of reality. We need to recover the ability to see every event as a potential window into mystery.

Loren Eiseley, an American anthropologist, was an elegant witness to our ability to find the extraordinary *within* the ordinary events of human knowing. He insisted that all human knowing, *even technology*, can be a vehicle of the Spirit. The inner world of experience is not to be confined to the sight of a sunset over the Rockies or water fowl rising in the morning mist. We need to include a beautiful piece of sculpture and a machine that works. We need to understand that technology as much as nature is grounded in the mystery of energy.

From time to time the church remembers its obscure heroes like Brother Lawrence, a seventeenth-century Carmelite mystic, who described how washing dishes in a monastery is an act of prayer. By that he meant that we need to comprehend the mystery that pervades *all* of life, whatever be our given task or place of service.

An eminent pathologist was speaking to a group of students. This leader in medical science was asked how he reconciled his Christian belief and his scientific study of disease. His reply was that it presented no problems. Six days a week he was a pathologist and on Sunday he was a Christian.

We are suggesting that the necessary rediscovery of the sacred means that whatever has implications—be it pathology, romance philology, dishwashing, insurance selling, stock brokering, or work on an automobile assembly line— can only be resolved in an awareness of the sacred nature of all of life. This does *not* imply there is a "Christian pathology" or a "Christian insurance selling" as opposed to some non-Christian counterpart. *It means that no human endeavor can ever be fully understood by humans. Mystery is inevitable wherever we live and work.*

We are not suggesting that everything is sacred in the sense that everything is in union with God. There is sin and it abounds. There is the absence of God in our thoughts and actions. There are destructive forces that fill our lives and tear us to pieces. We are simply stating our conviction that no human experience is, in the final analysis, to be explained by purely secular (nontranscendent) categories. All of life emerges out of an unfathomable mystery, a mystery which becomes apparent when we seek to understand its full implications. Everything we know about our experience has on the "edge" of that knowledge unanswered questions.

The proper purpose then of sacred places, events, and things is to focus our attention on the sacred, which pervades all things, to hold the sacred before us and to call us to live accordingly. For example, God does not "live" in the church building. God is not confined to a place or hour. The presence of Christ is not confined to the bread and wine of the Eucharist. But we have churches and liturgies for the same reason we observe the Fourth of July, celebrate birthdays, share a formal dinner, or give a gold watch at retirement. Without the specific designation of certain places, events, and things we would lose contact with what transcends the immediate moment or the surface appearance.

It is similar to the functions of a priest. The act of priesting can be and indeed is performed by all of us. That is what we mean by the priesthood of all believers. But the priest is the one called by the community to illuminate the priest in all of us. Without priests we would not know of our common priesthood. The purpose of one set aside and identified as a priest is to point to the priest in us all. The purpose of the Eucharist is to transform every meal into a holy moment.

Of course, all identification of the general in the particular can be demonic. We can give, for example, an objective existence to the priest over against a universal priesthood. But to do that is to separate the sacred and the profane. By maintaining the secular within our consciousness we seek to avoid the tyranny of the sacred which has plagued humanity; but this impulse has caused some people to revolt and try to destroy the sacred altogether. The price of this attempt has been devastating to the human spirit.

Our modern American ideology has unconsciously engulfed us all. It is founded on a worldly salvation; it is positivistic, individualistic, and stresses the relationship of human beings to objects over the relationship of human beings to each other. It focuses on a this-worldly instrumentalism as the solution of all problems, assuming that if our technology is able to produce sufficient wealth and power all our problems will be solved. While claiming to be neutral and objective, it fosters materialism.

Traditional religion, on the other hand, defines human fulfillment as bringing human life into harmony with the holy and the good. Traditional religion asserts limits and finitude to the human condition. Yet it has always served equality and justice as an overreaching set of values that link God, or ultimate reality, to the cosmos and to the individual soul.

All of us must live—if we are to live at all—by beliefs, attitudes, and values—and so we are confronted today by the problem of believing and belief in an alien context. The challenge, however, must be met. Humans have no choice.

Living for Values

Believers witness by the style of their lives to their beliefs. This is one consequence of belief. A second consequence of belief, related to the first, is that we all live for values. By values we mean a cluster of meaning, independent of our own whims, in which we have a sufficiently deep investment that, if necessary, we will change the patterns of our lives or even surrender our earthly life for its sake.

Believers in their experience of the sacred dimension of life find a moral demand placed upon them. This is inevitable. God is, by definition, the source of order. Purposeful living

is to live for the vision of that order. We validate our behavior as individuals and as a people ultimately by appealing
to a cosmic order, *which is given.* It is not something we
create for the sake of expediency. It is there for us to live by,
discovered in the awareness of the sacred. Therefore, we
expect from the sacred a legitimation of the good and a condemnation of the bad.

But try, for example, explaining to your son or your
daughter in a secular vacuum, where appeals to sacred sanctions are tacitly or explicitly invalidated, why you find casual
sexual relations repugnant. You know that something about
it does violence "to the order of things," but a failure to share
a common value, that is grounded in the sacred dimension of
the sexual relationship, makes the argument futile. All that
we can do is appeal to duty—"We just do not do that kind of
thing."

Duty is all that remains when we lose a sense of value. It is
the only moral guide left for a people who have divided the
sacred from the profane and still wish to control human behavior; it is the only moral guide for a secular society which
does not desire the collapse of all norms for social conduct.
This appeal to duty rather than value even invaded the
church. Even the Offices of Instruction in the 1928 *Book of
Common Prayer* were long on a sense of duty. "My bounden
duty is to" is the beginning of every answer to the questions
placed before the people.

Until the present, every edition of the *Book of Common
Prayer* since the sixteenth century has been strongly influenced by a notion of God, which makes a radical division
between the sacred and the profane. It is significant, however, that the new *Prayer Book,* while speaking of the love for
God, has no mention in its catechism of *duty.* Whereas moral
chaos—"every-person-for-him-or-herself"—is a collapse
into the less than human, duty is a holding action. It demands that we live by collective expectations and asks only
acceptance. "Ours not to reason why, ours but to do or die."
As a holding action it either presumes that the Kingdom of
God has arrived and is embodied in the present social con-
tract, or it cannot find the courage to make provision for a

deeper understanding of the divine moral imperative to live beyond our duty.

If we live by values, however, we are suggesting that the sense of morality is evolving. It emerges out of the continuing experience of a personal God who sanctions or legitimates our life. It is the demand that an interpersonal relationship in which we not only find meaning but the promise of personal fulfillment lays upon us. Our values are an expression of a deepening relationship that promotes wholeness, and our action is the result of a desire to do nothing that violates the possibility of becoming more human in relation.

It appears that St. Paul's well-known injunction to the Christians at Corinth is best understood in the light of these comments: " . . . the written code kills, but the Spirit gives life" (II Cor. 3:6). The Corinthians were giving Paul a hard time and wanted him to show his credentials. His reply was to say that written credentials are stultifying. It is in the experience of the other within our heart that is the appropriate ground of God's claim upon us. Paul was not advocating lawlessness. He was saying that the law is never enough. The Christian lives for more: the values that emerge in the experience of the Spirit of God.

A value is an enduring belief that a specific mode of conduct or good for life is both personally and socially desirable.

A value system suggests a rank-ordering of values along a continuum of importance. Typically situations confront us in which two or more of our values are in conflict with one another. For example, we may have to choose between the goal of freedom or equality, between behaving truthfully or patriotically. We cannot do both simultaneously. When this occurs, the value we have placed highest in our scale of values will determine our action.

Once a value is internalized it becomes, consciously or unconsciously, a standard or criterion for guiding action, for framing attitudes, and for making moral judgments. A value is more than a belief about what is preferable; it is an imperative to action.

Why then is forgiveness a supreme Christian value? Forgiveness is made the condition of healing in the Gospels (Mt. 9:2). Peter is told by Jesus that he must forgive those who sin against him an infinite number of times (Mt. 18:21). In the prayer Jesus taught his disciples, we ask, "Forgive us our sins as we forgive those who sin against us." From the Cross itself Jesus forgave his executors (Lk. 23:34). The answer lies in the Christian experience of that sin which has to be overcome if wholeness is to be present. Sin is what violates the unity of all things in God—the pervading expectation of the Christian vision of life. If we are to embody the Gospel, we must forgive as God forgives. Without forgiveness there is no grace or presence, no unity.

We speak of forgiveness as a "supreme Christian value." Obviously this implies a hierarchy or ordering of values. Some values take precedence over others. For example, responsibility is an important value. One ought to be responsible. The question comes up: Does one forgive someone who is irresponsible? What takes precedence: forgiveness or responsibility?

In the way of an illustration, one recalls a woman who had a career as an accountant. Her son was killed as a passenger in an automobile accident in which a friend of his, driving while intoxicated, came out untouched. The woman felt great anger at the survivor, particularly since he suffered little at the hands of the law. She had once been strongly opposed to "organized religion." Some time after her son's death she herself was involved in a situation where, through an error on her part, the company for which she worked as accountant suffered a severe financial loss. As a result she was brought face to face with her need to hold her son's friend responsible for his tragic death and her desire for forgiveness for her own error. She went through a period of traumatic self-examination, which resulted in not only enabling her to forgive the person whom she previously felt was responsible for her son's death, but also opened her to the faith and belief of the Christian community.

Our suspicion is that the conversion of St. Paul involves a

similar dynamic where his admiration of the purity of the hearts of those Christians whom he had once persecuted, as in the martyrdom of Stephen (Acts 8:1), conflicted with his zeal for orthodoxy. The vision on the road to Damascus was the first step in the resolution of that conflict and the opening of Paul to the experience of God in Christ (Acts 9:1—9).

To live for values which express the sacred dimension of all life leads us to conclude that all life has value. This is particularly applicable to a priestly vocation. Not infrequently, converts to a Christian understanding of the experience of God will seek ordination to the priesthood on the basis that they now must give their lives to God's service.

We might suppose that previously they were in newspaper work or in business. Their assumption is that in the eyes of God working on a newspaper or being a salesperson has no value. We would hold, however, that to the extent that it is an authentic human service, all work has value as great as that of being a priest. All life participates in the source of life and therefore all that serves life has value.

The Christian style of life, growing out of Christian faith and belief, is one that possesses an awareness of the sacred and is guided by a commitment to values that transcend social expectations.

All human action takes place within the context of our conception of life's meaning. Questions about morality always point to questions about faith. How people act depends on their vision of human life and its significance, their vision of the world and its fulfillment. If we turn this concept around, we may say that our visions and our values imply deeds. More simply, Christian faith expresses itself in action.

Each day we must make decisions and accept the consequences of our action or inaction. Each day, then, we confront the question of life's meaning and the world's purpose. Even small actions are indicative of fundamental values. The question of faith is always inescapable. Faced with a decision for action we must make up our minds about what to do and hence about what we believe about life and its significance.

The words of Jesus were a call to sincere and resolute deeds of love toward all peoples. If we do not act accordingly we have no right to the name disciple. "Why do you call me 'Lord, Lord' and do not do what I tell you?" (Lk. 6:46.)

James wrote, "But someone will say 'You have faith and I have works.' Show me your faith apart from your works, and I by my works will show you my faith."(Jas. 2:18.)

The life of Christ is a lesson in responsibility. God has offered us a new possibility for personal and corporate life. It is our responsibility to affirm that possibility by acting accordingly. Yet instead of assuming responsibility we accuse God of not working in the world. But it is not God that is absent; we are absent. Instead of wondering why God allows people to starve, we need to examine why we allow people to hunger and thirst. We are to work in the world for God's purposes through the power of the Holy Spirit. Then God is glorified and our lives made whole. The gift of grace and the Spirit have set us free. Because we are free, we are free to live and work for others.

When we speak of a "personal relationship with Jesus Christ," we are speaking of a calling to witness for justice, peace, equality, liberation, community, and the well-being of all peoples. Our relationship with Christ demands that we never fall victim to life as it is.

Margaret Mead, a while ago, was recounting her days in New Guinea. She shared one of the stories told by the people. It went like this:

> Originally Jesus of Nazareth spoke so that everyone could understand him, without figures of speech that obscure the meaning. But the Pharisees and the Saducees got together (the New Guinea people are not quite sure when this happened in time) and obscured what Jesus had said and made it difficult to understand. Then the ecclesiastics of the Christian Church got together and divided the truth up and gave a little bit to the Presbyterians, a little bit to the Seventh Day Adventists, a little bit to the Catholics; so that *nobody* could understand what was being said. And the Lord God said, "What am I going to do? What am I going to do about New Guinea? I sent the English and they weren't any good. I sent the Germans and they weren't any good. I sent the Americans, they weren't too bad, but they wouldn't stay—they went home again." And then the Lord God said, "There's nothing to do but ask the people of New Guinea themselves to take charge."

That is the sad tale of how Christianity came to New Guinea. Then she explained how she returned to New Guinea where five years before Catholics and Protestants had been screaming judgment at each other in a village where people had never before heard a voice raised. Now the lion was lying down with the lamb. They had all become ecumenical. They were all talking to each other and nobody was shouting anymore, and they all came to see her at once to discuss the problems of the relationship between their missions and the local natives' beliefs.

She sat there, temporarily exhilarated. There were two nuns, there was a priest, there was lively and inspired Protestant leadership, and they said: "On the whole we have decided that we don't have anything to tell these people. We had better leave them with their own religion and go home." She looked at them, because she knew something about these people. She knew that the height of their religious experience was an allegiance to the special guardian ghosts and spirits of their own little village, something they couldn't share with anybody in the world. And she said: "Do you really think that you don't have anything to give?" They said: "Well, no! I think maybe we had better leave them as they are."

What had happened is that these people did not go to New Guinea to make Christians, but they went to New Guinea to be sure the Roman Catholics didn't get them, or that the Protestants didn't get them, or that the Seventh Day Adventists didn't get them. Once they were robbed of their competitiveness, they had nothing left. And they were going home. The only people who, as a group, were not going home were the sisters. The sisters came to care for the widowed and the helpless and the orphaned and the sick. They had no doubts as to why they were there. And they had no desire to leave. They may have changed their habits into more modern attire, but they had not changed their motivation.

It matters what we believe. It matters how we believe. It matters what values we hold. It matters what vision has captured our imaginations. It matters why we live and for what we live.

Other volumes which follow in this new Church's Teaching Series will explore the Bible, the church in history, Christian understanding, sacramental living, Christian moral life, and life in the spirit. We trust that we have given good and solid reasons for the serious study of our Christian faith and life. More important, we hope we have provided the Christian community of faith with an apologetic for Christian belief and believing in our day of false belief, nonbelief, and disbelief.

We share a common human longing for meaning and purpose; we know we do not live by bread alone. We search for truth and knowledge. We have been given the gift of faith and we seek to share our faith with others. We are never an island unto ourselves. We need one another. There is a worldwide hunger, almost frightening in its intensity, for it suggests something akin to starvation. It is a hunger for what in an old phrase was called "newness of life." This book was written to feed that hunger. It is, therefore, dedicated to all who sense the relationship of what and how we believe to what we are, to all those who accept the consequences of belief, especially those who have come to know the truth of God's converting revelation in Jesus Christ and who in these days strive to be faithful.

Suggestions
for Further Reading

The following books are suggested for further reading for the volume *Christian Believing:* Robert McAfee Brown, *Is Faith Obsolete?* (Westminster Press, 1974), Louis Dupré, *The Other Dimension* (Seabury Press, paperback, 1979), Philip Greven, *The Protestant Temperment* (Alfred A. Knopf, 1977), Ray Hart, *Unfinished Man and the Imagination* (Seabury Press, paperback, 1979), Urban T. Holmes III, *To Speak of God* (Seabury Press, 1974), and Bernard Lonergan, *Method in Theology* (Seabury Press, paperback, 1979). *Understanding the Faith of the Church*, a volume in the Church's Teaching Series, by Richard Norris (Seabury Press, 1979) is recommended as is Karl Rahner's *Foundations of Christian Faith* (Seabury Press, 1978). Elizabeth Sewell's *The Human Metaphor* (University of Notre Dame Press, 1963), while out of print, could be obtained from a library. Other recommended books are *Belief and History* by Wildred Cantwell Smith (University Press of Virginia, 1977), *Ways of Being Religious* by Frederick J. Streng, Charles Lloyd, and Jay Allen (Prentice Hall, 1973), and *Blessed Rage for Order* by David Tracy (Seabury Press, 1975).

Index